Springer Series on

ADULTHOOD and AGING

Volume 1:
Adult Day Care
Community Work with the Elderly
Philip G. Weiler and Eloise Rathbone-McCuan
with contributors

Volume 2:
Counseling Elders and Their Families
Practical Techniques for Applied Gerontology
John J. Herr and John H. Weakland

Volume 3:
Becoming Old
An Introduction to Social Gerontology
John C. Morgan

Volume 4:
The Projective Assessment of Aging Method (PAAM)
Bernard D. Starr, Marcella Bakur Weiner,
and Marilyn Rabetz

Volume 5:
Ethnicity and Aging
Donald E. Gelfand and Alfred E. Kutzik
with 25 contributors

John C. Morgan, M.A., has over ten years experience in planning community development programs. In addition to teaching at the community college level, he has been a statewide training coordinator in gerontology and the executive director of the Senior Citizens Association of Lorain County (Ohio), which was selected as the top senior citizens' program in the United States in 1978 by the National Association of Counties. Currently he is the chief planner for a home care corporation serving older persons in Massachusetts. He is also the author of *The Psychology of Death and Dying,* published in 1977.

BECOMING OLD

An Introduction to Social Gerontology

John C. Morgan

SPRINGER PUBLISHING COMPANY
New York

Springer Publishing Company, Inc.
200 Park Avenue South
New York, N.Y. 10003

79 80 81 82 83 / 10 9 8 7 6 5 4 3 2 1

Library of Congress Cataloging in Publication Data

Morgan, John Crossley, 1941–
Becoming old

(Springer series on adulthood and aging; v. 3)
Includes bibliographies and index.
1. Gerontology—United States. 2. Aged—Psychology. 3. Social work with the aged—United States. I. Title. II. Series.
HQ1064.U5M68 362.6'042'0973 79-558
ISBN 0-8261-2620-0
ISBN 0-8261-2621-9 pbk.

Printed in the United States of America

To my friends of the Senior Citizens Association of Lorain County, Ohio, whose experiences provided much of the background for the development of this book; and for my father, who refuses to be a "senior citizen."

CONTENTS

PREFACE

Each one of us begins to age from the moment of birth. If this seems a self-evident fact of life, it is nonetheless one which often eludes our understanding, perhaps because most tend to think of growing old as a negative process to be avoided. How we age depends on many factors, not the least of which is our own individual developmental pattern over a lifetime. But of particular importance are the social forces that influence the later years of life in relation to each individual. Persons may adapt to these forces from past behavior or with new insights, but the society in which individuals age plays a strategic role in self-perception and self-esteem.

Individuals do adapt successfully to the aging process, perhaps far more so than is commonly assumed. However, the social environment does not always promote successful aging and may, in fact, hamper continued growth in the later years of life. For example, while older persons may desire to continue their vocations past retirement years, until recently this was not possible. Persons were required to retire at a certain age or, if they continued working, were penalized in terms of reduced retirement benefits.

In writing this book I have intended to focus primarily on the social forces involved in aging, although not without some introductory materials on the biological and clinical aspects of growing old. Of particular importance to me has been the need to come to grips with the social factors of later life, and then to relate the analysis of these factors to what is feasible and desirable in the reformation of social environments.

There is nothing more practical than a good theory—at least this is the argument of social philosophers. On the other hand, those who work in the field of aging become frustrated with social philosophers who cannot understand the paradoxes of bureaucracies and the day-to-day problems of social planning. There is now a growing awareness of the need for a meeting ground between those involved in research in aging and those involved in developing and providing services to older adults. Because the field of gerontology is still relatively new, as is the development of community services for older persons, the meeting ground is not clearly defined. One of the major objectives of this book is to provide a bridge between the worlds of theory and practice, with the assumption that both worlds will benefit from the exchange.

My goal has been to produce a resource book for those considering careers in the field of aging. Much of the material in the book is directly applicable to persons who wish to work with older persons in many of the new fields associated with aging. As the percentage of the United States population 60 years of age and older continues to increase, there will be more demand for sensitive and skilled social workers, planners, administrators, outreach workers, geriatric nurses, and other community-service professionals.

This book will also aid those already involved in the planning and administering of programs for older adults, and those older citizens who serve as members of boards of directors or advisory councils. To a greater extent than may be desirable, younger persons tend to become the directors and planners of programs in the field of aging; but older citizens are most frequently called upon to act as policy makers at the community level. Hopefully, this book will provide them with the information required in the performance of their responsibilities.

For those who wish to study social gerontology in more detail, an appendix has been included herein to suggest other resources available, including periodicals, organizations for older adults, articles on special subjects, case studies, films and audiotapes, and activities related to each chapter.

Whatever the shortcomings of this book, it has been my goal to provide a realistic picture of the problems and possibilities of becoming old in society. I would be remiss if I did not acknowledge my rich—and sometimes frustrating—experiences as the executive director of a nonprofit corporation for older persons in Lorain County, Ohio. I could not have gained such knowledge from books alone. My experiences at this level of the aging network have only increased my belief in the possibility of reforming social structures, even with the resources and skills now available.

BECOMING OLD

An Introduction to Social Gerontology

1

Becoming Old with Dignity

An Overview of Aging

One cannot understand the meaning of growing old without first coming to terms with one's own humanity and with the meaning of history; to age is to participate in the humanity in which all persons share. At every moment of life each person ages, although few are aware of this process until they pass into that stage of life known as "old age." There are indications, moreover, that even having passed a certain age—say, 65 years old—persons may not consider themselves old, but instead identify with life-styles and values of individuals 20 years younger.

What does it mean to age? This question must be addressed from various standpoints. First, in terms of biological development, what happens to the human body over time as it ages? Second, in terms of personal development, what perceptions, feelings, and values (if any) can be said to be common to aging persons? And third, in a broader social context, what are the social forces that set the wider context in which persons grow old? The title of this book, *Becoming Old,* indicates it is the response to the third question that is crucial to the practice of gerontology at the community level, although this does not imply that either the personal or biological dimensions of aging can be dismissed as unworthy of examination. The processes of aging are interrelated, and there are ample examples of work now being carried out in basic research and personality development, but the search for the community aspects of aging has just begun. Understanding that aging is a process of individual growth over time is vital to any interpretation. Such growth takes place in relationships, in the close ties of the family, and in communities and whole cultures.

The systematic study of aging is a recent development. Gerontology, which means literally the "science of aging," is a new scientific endeavor and encompasses the work of biologists, sociologists, psychologists, philosophers, and social workers. The increase in the percentage of older persons in Western Civilization has, in part, led to this increased interest. One need only compare the average longevity of the modern age with that of past epochs to understand how dramatically the age groupings have changed. Life expectancy in the Roman Empire was 23 years; in New England about 1850 life expectancy was 40 years; at the turn of the century in this country it was 47 years; and today life duration is over 70 years.

Two sociological categories related to status might better explain the meaning of aging in the modern world: *ascribed status* and *achieved status.* Ascribed status is attached to a person because of sex, race, class, or age. Achieved status is given a person because of accomplishments. Because persons age, there will probably always be an element of ascribed status in growing old; a person 80 years old is seen differently from a 20-year-old college student, even though both may share certain common qualities such as taste in music or life values. Modern history has brought about a shift from ascribed to achieved status; persons are supposedly given access to status by their accomplishments, at least in more industrialized countries. Yet, with regard to older persons, the concept of achieved status is more difficult to assess. As long as persons past a certain age are denied the freedom to participate in those activities that lead to accomplishments, a great deal of personal insecurity and anguish will result. For example, if a culture places a high premium on the values of work and lends status to those who have achieved in this dimension, it becomes extremely difficult for an older individual who has been forced to retire to attain such status. It is not clear whether ascribed status is a positive factor in modern life during later years. One might argue that old age is a time for reflection and concern for the next generation, and this can certainly be the case. One could argue equally, however, that in highly industrialized societies, older persons are seen as economic burdens since they are relegated to the nonworking and become more dependent on services rather than being producers themselves.

Aging in a Social Context

The concept of an older population in need of systematic societal intervention is one of recent origin in American society. This is not to imply that the status of older persons was not addressed in other cultures and ages. It is extremely difficult to write a history of aging, simply because older persons were not considered subjects worthy of special mention or were not considered at all because they did not exist in significant numbers in society. One could catch images of growing old in literature, in the plays of Shakespeare for example, but often the pictures were of comic characters or individuals held up for pity. In some cases, such as portions of the Old Testament or in Chinese culture, one might find portrayals of older persons as wise elders to whom a community turned for guidance in times of turmoil. But the recognition that aging was a problem to be solved by "society" is of very recent origin in American history.

Just as other intellectual disciplines—e.g., philosophy, theology, science—turned during the later part of the nineteenth century toward a growing awareness of their social requirements, so too was there a new concern for the social improvement of the lot of older persons. In the early 1900s a number of developments heralded this view. In 1909 Massachusetts named the first public commission on older persons in the United States; the first old-age pension system was established in Arizona in 1915; and some of the first early texts on aging were printed during this same period. Not only were persons becoming aware of issues surrounding aging, but, more important, scientific principles were being applied to the resolution of social concerns. Americans were by now already behind in their concern; European countries had already explored the problems and come up with tentative solutions, such as mandatory old-age insurance in Germany at the end of the nineteenth century. America was not without pensions, for many Civil War veterans did receive benefits, but all others were generally excluded.

It was not until the 1920s that legislation related to old age began to be of national concern. In the face of the Depression of the 1930s, it became obvious that few older citizens were adequately covered by any kind of pension plan. One of the more interesting proposals to come out of this period was that of Dr. Francis Townsend, who at the age of 67 proposed the establishment of an old-age pension plan for everyone over 60 years of age. The plan, financed by a sales tax, was to provide $150 a month for older persons, provided they spent the money as they received it. Townsend's plan took on the semblance of a religious crusade. The attempt to convert the plan into law failed, but the movement highlighted the need for action.

The first nationally important piece of legislation for old age insurance, the Social Security Act, was enacted in 1935; it remains one of the most significant pieces of legislation ever passed for older persons in the United States. It was not enacted, however, without criticism. Townsend found it to be generally inadequate to meet the needs of older persons, while others attacked its lack of health insurance or the uncertain administrative provisions for carrying out the requirements of the law. The Supreme Court, by a single vote, declared the Act consistent with the Constitution.

The Paradox of Aging

In early America, perhaps under a religious influence, there was a general feeling of respect for older persons. Sermons and religious tracts provide examples of this attitude, and many older persons, such as Benjamin Franklin, remained leaders in the Colonial period. To be sure, few persons reached ages that today might be considered old. It has been estimated that less than 2 percent of the American population in the early years of the Republic were 65 years of age or older. Infant mortality, inadequate health care, and the rigors of life did not provide environments for longevity. In the midst of territorial expansion and the development of new forms of government, older persons provided stability and leadership in officeholding and the organization of new communities.

Around the turn of the nineteenth century, a change of attitude can be detected toward older persons, perhaps due in part to the emphasis upon work and achievement and new economic realities. Perhaps more important than economics was the fact that the percentage of older persons in the general population was increasing. In 1790, for example, the median age of the American population was 16 (which means that 50 percent of the persons alive were 16 years of age or younger), but in 1870 the median age was 20, and in 1920 it was 25.

Adaptation to this new social reality—the increased percentage of older persons in the general population—remains at the heart of the paradox of aging in America.

Aging: Loss and Reestablishment

The process of aging can be seen in terms of the sudden or gradual loss of status in society and of self-esteem in personal relationships. The fear of aging is related to the apprehension of these losses.

These negative aspects of aging may become internalized by older persons, causing them to succumb to the role expectations of others. When age becomes the single category for locating status in a society, ageism tends to arise. The attitude of ageism can dehumanize individuals by allowing them to be judged solely on the basis of their age. For example, a company may set a mandatory retirement age of 65, with little thought given to whether or not persons this age or over can and want to work. The individual thus becomes subject to a policy, and no exceptions to the general rule are permitted.

Many activists in the field of aging have adopted an agenda of confrontation with what they consider to be ageist policies; most especially under attack in recent years has been the issue of mandatory retirement, with the result that federal legislation has been directed toward easing the age restrictions governing retirement.

Although aging can be viewed under the general theme of loss, it can also be seen in terms of reestablishment. The simple fact remains that many older persons are successful agers, often in spite of the societal restrictions involved.

Because the negative stereotypes of growing old are prevalent in contemporary society, it is important to grasp the significance of the fact that older persons also find ways to adapt and grow within the later years of life. A few examples of successful aging are presented here; these are based on real-life cases.

Case 1. Mr. Jones is 74 years old and has been retired for nine years. He maintains an active involvement in community affairs and is, as he admits, "more busy now than ever." In addition to being president of a housing authority board, on a welfare council, and involved with a local church, he has taken a new interest in programs for older persons and helped to initiate a nonprofit corporation to provide services. Along with these volunteer activities, Mr. Jones works part-time under a government employment program as the editor of a newspaper for retired persons. His advice is constantly sought by others in positions of community leadership.

Case 2. Miss Smith is nearing retirement, but continues to work full-time as the coordinator of a nutrition program for older persons. Her work involves both administrative and counseling skills. For many years, long before the advent of government programs, she managed food service projects for older citizens in public housing projects. Her interests span the generations, as evidenced by her ability in starting day-care centers for children.

Case 3. Mr. Kline is 75 years old, and in his own words is "enjoying life now more than ever." He is a political activist, fully aware of the voting power of older citizens, who spends weeks researching issues, attending public hearings, and lobbying for the interests of consumers. Almost single-handedly at times he has argued for consumer rights, most especially in the area of public utilities.

Case 4. Mrs. Jacob continues her lifelong work as a caseworker, although she is no longer employed full-time. In addition to serving on various community boards, she spearheaded a drive to begin nutrition programs throughout her region. In her spare time she works as a volunteer providing home services to older adults.

Case 5. Mr. Lewis sees himself as a consumer advocate and a gadfly. A retired teacher, he considers the world his classroom. His involvement has led to many consumer programs throughout the region.

Are these persons unique? Probably not, especially since they all live in one small county; their examples could be duplicated across the country.

The Potential of the Later Years

The later years of life are characterized by both continuity and change. Individuals may tend to adapt more successfully to aging if throughout life they have found ways to cope with living. The key element is that of adaptation—how persons make adjustments over time to new personal and social conditions. But in order to make adjustments, freedom of choice remains a powerful positive force. Self-esteem may, to a large extent, be shaped by how much power an individual perceives he or she possesses over events and situations.

Growing old with dignity, therefore, may mean rather simply the promotion of development, based on the element of choice. Individuals who learn to adapt, and who perceive a measure of self-dignity arising from personal choice, will tend to age successfully.

2

Stereotypes and Realities of Aging

What Does It Mean To Be Old?

At what time is a person considered old? This question remains relevant, although many suppose the answer to be easy. Some persons might think that to be old involves certain physical characteristics—gray hair, wrinkles—but then how is one to categorize younger individuals who may appear aged prematurely? Other individuals might argue instead that aging is a chronological point in time. But the difficulty of this assumption is in specifying at exactly what point an individual becomes old. For example, the common indicators of chronological age are themselves confusing: the Older Americans Act requires that only persons 60 years of age and older be considered old; retirement laws often take effect at the age of 65; Social Security benefits may begin at age 62; and some voluntary associations for older persons open membership to those 55 years of age and older. Both the physical and chronological assessments of aging are external to the process of growing old; that is, by common agreement and societal approval a definition of what it means to be old may be created.

Are there, then, any internal definitions of what it means to be old? Is there any time at which a person believes himself or herself to be old? Once again, it is difficult to make any statement that cannot be refuted. It has already been noted that for some persons, regardless of age, there is no personal identity with old age.

Studies have shown that older adults may identify with the values and life-styles of much younger age groups and do not consider themselves "old" even if chronological age makes them eligible for retirement. In fact, on more than one occasion, persons well into their 70s have been known to resent being called old. In one senior center program, for example, a social worker attempting to interest an older man in the activities was curtly put off by the comment: "What do I have in common with those old fogies?"

The attempt to arrive at an acceptable definition of what it means to be old is, of course, useful for societal purposes. Whole social service systems, such as Social Security, are based on the assumption of old age, and support systems are developed from such indicators. But great care must be taken in applying any general definitions of what it means to be old to every person, for there are vast individual differences which simply will not fit into general principles. One helpful attitude to adopt is that of recognizing that aging is a normal and continuous process from the moment of birth; growing old therefore comes to be seen as a process of becoming, of developing over time. By understanding this view it is also possible to attain some measure of sympathy for those in the later years of life, because they are mirrors of a process already at work within ourselves.

The Stereotypes of Aging

Social stratification, a characteristic of all human societies and observed by scientists in all communities to some extent since the beginning of recorded history, is a cultural pattern that illustrates the human desire for power, prestige, and privilege. Two broad approaches have been developed in contemporary thought to explain why social stratification exists. The first might be called the "power theory" and suggests that stratification takes place in the exercise of power in social life. A second approach might be called the "functional theory"; from this vantage point, stratification exists because it serves a beneficial purpose in the social order. Persons may be stratified in the social order by class, race, and income, as well as by age. It is with this analysis in mind that the question of stereotypes must be seen, for stereotypes may be viewed as systematic patterns of beliefs and values—some negative and others positive—which have the purpose of furthering social stratification.

There are many examples of stereotypes in the field of aging, but some of the more prevalent are addressed here as a means of exploring their hold on our common imaginations.

1. *Once retired, persons are finally able to enjoy life fully, without the pressures of day-to-day living.* As with all stereotypes, there is some measure of truth in this common view, for many older persons, particularly those who have planned ahead for retirement, do find a new opportunity to pursue interests. For many others, however, with retirement also comes social, economic, and personal dislocation. Income certainly shrinks, and even when persons have saved for retirement, the cost of goods and services sharply reduces the value of savings. In the United States in 1971, for example, according to the Bureau of Labor Statistics, about 22 percent of those in their retirement years had annual incomes below established poverty levels; with regard to single individuals, about half were living off annual incomes of between $1,000 and $5,000.
2. *The older individual is basically a conservative, conformist member of society.* This stereotype is rooted in the familiar saying, "you can't teach an old dog new tricks." The argument that older persons wish to conserve time and money in order to adapt to retirement is carried one step further by stating that aged individuals also conserve ideas and values and are rigid in outlook and behavior. Political and social values, however, tend to remain fairly within the middle-of-the-road position among older persons.
3. *The number of years a person lives correlates with his or her knowledge; thus, older persons will tend to be wiser than younger persons.* In some non-Western cultures the position of the older person is held in more esteem than in America. Wisdom is equated with long life. It should be clear, however, that wisdom is not a quality evident among all older persons, nor is it their special gift. If this were the case, wisdom could be measured simply by the number of years lived rather than by the insight displayed.
4. *Most older persons are institutionalized.* The stereotype of the institutionalized older adult, most especially confined to a nursing home, is still held by many. This stereotype might explain why community leaders often find it easier to rally support for nursing home residents than for older citizens in their own homes. At present the estimate of persons 65 years of age and older who are institutionalized is from 5 to 8 percent of the aged population.

5. *Old age is a second childhood.* Old age can be seen as corresponding roughly to a second childhood. Older persons, particularly those who appear frail, are referred to as "dear," "sweet," or "cute"—terms usually reserved for infants. Yet these terms violate the dignity of the person, for they deny the full range of emotions and actions to those past a certain age.

Stereotypes are a social means by which persons are placed in certain groupings. However, when stereotypes are so rigid that no individual differences are permitted, a destructive process is set in motion. If all older adults are seen to be happy in their retirement years, for example, then little effort will to be made to alleviate the plight of those who are living in poverty. If it is natural for older persons to be institutionalized, then no effort will be made to support programs to assist older adults in remaining within their own homes and communities. Rigid stereotypes deny the full range of human differences and hence the promise of continued growth in the later years of life.

The Realities of Aging

Various generalizations about the older adult population in the United States can be made on the basis of demographic research. Of course, one must permit for a wide variation of individual behavior within these general statements.

1. *Most older persons remain within a family setting.* The overwhelming majority of persons 65 and over still live in their own homes; only one in 20 resides in an institutional setting. Unfortunately, much past research has been concentrated on older persons who are institutionalized, but a new emphasis has been placed on understanding those older adults who live independently within their own communities.
2. *A significant proportion of older persons live below established poverty levels.* In 1970, one in every four older persons lived below established government poverty levels. Of the over 7 million families with heads of household over 65 years of age, half had incomes less than $5,000 annually. Of particular concern is the plight of older women; in 1970, 51 percent of older females living alone had incomes that were below the poverty line. In addition, many of these women

were employed only infrequently during their working years, and thus were dependent upon their husbands for economic self-sufficiency. Since a 1973 change in the Social Security law, widows receive the full amount that their spouses received in benefits. Minority groups appear to suffer most from income deprivation.

3. *The number and proportion of persons in the later stages of life is dramatically increasing in the United States.* The population of the United States increased by about 100 percent from 1900 to 1950; the population of persons 65 and over during the same period increased by 300 percent. Approximately one in every 10 Americans is 65 or over, and by the year 2000 it is predicted that at least 28 million persons will be in this age bracket. Each year the number of people 65 and older in this country increases by 365,000.
4. *The percentage of persons who are older but continue to work full-time continues to decline.* Less than one in every five persons who are older continues to work. Mandatory retirement, age discrimination in hiring, and federal regulations all hamper continued employment during the later years. For example, in 1977 persons on Social Security could earn up to $3,000 annually without losing other federal benefits.
5. *Governmental responses to the problems of aging remain fragmented.* There is as yet no unified federal response to the problems of aging. The Federal Administration on Aging is not a Cabinet-level department but part of the massive Department of Health, Education and Welfare. Funding under the Older Americans Act remains limited, and guidelines change regularly. Federal benefits do not keep pace with the increased cost of living. One case in point might illustrate this inadequacy. As a result of a 5 percent increase in Social Security, an older woman who lived in city public housing encountered the following: her rent was increased in public housing because she was placed in a new income category; she was told by social service workers that she was no longer eligible for Food Stamps; a private agency withdrew homemaker services because she was no longer "poor." In all, the "increase" reduced her monthly income by 10 percent. No wonder then, that she could remark: "Medical science has made it possible to live longer, and economics has made it impossible to survive."

3

The Psychology of Aging

Approaches to Behavior in the Later Years

Persons age at different rates. There are consequently many approaches to the study of behavior among older adults. James Birren, director of the University of Southern California's Ethel Percy Andrus Gerontology Center, outlines four perspectives from which behavior in aging adults may be explored.[1]

1. Behavior may be studied by observing the rate at which information is received and transmitted. Over time, individuals tend to store more and more information based on their life experiences; however, the ability to recall this information tends to decrease with time as well. Nonetheless, older persons may be able to conceptualize problems from past issues faced; not as much intellectual energy need be wasted in investigation since there is a storehouse of data available.
2. Behavior in the later years may also be viewed from the framework of longevity. Why do some people live so long? There are no conclusive answers to this question, but there are some indicators that may provide guidelines. Heredity may play a part in how long a person lives; females tend to live longer lives than males. Other factors that have impact on longevity include nutrition, environmental factors, and economic conditions.
3. A third approach to the study of behavior in the later years is in relation to disease. About one-third of all persons 65 years of age and older in the United States suffer from one or more physical problems that have impact on behavior, the most common of which is heart disease.

4. The experience of aging is another perspective from which to study behavior. Aging can be interpreted as the internal experience of the individual. Each individual may experience aging in a different way. Some persons report little or no difficulty in growing old, while others find adaptation to the aging process difficult.

Some Views of Aging

Aging has been studied from a number of psychological perspectives, but only a few of the more prominent theories can be touched here. Ironically, Sigmund Freud never developed a comprehensive theory of aging, probably due to the fact that he did not believe psychoanalysis would be of special benefit to persons past the age of 40.

Carl Jung believed it was the fear of life, not death, which gripped the personality in the later years of existence. As persons age they become introspective and begin to withdraw from life. This withdrawal, Jung states, is a natural process. The crisis of the later years takes place when individuals, in reviewing their lives, do not believe they have attained their goals. Gradually the older person sinks back into the unconscious, a withdrawal from life.

Erich Fromm points out that entire cultures may set up conditions that lead some of its members to prefer death over life. One major factor that leads to the desire for death over life is the development of social situations that increase feelings of nonproductivity.

The famed psychologist Erik Erikson developed a series of eight stages of human growth. Each of these stages represents a duality—trust or distrust, autonomy of self-doubt—which causes persons to grow or not grow. If a person's ego grows to his or her benefit, he or she has successfully completed one stage of ego development and should be able to move to the next. However, if the individual is unsuccessful in adapting to the demands of the inner self as well as the outside world, he or she will not move into a new stage. Two of these ego stages are especially relevant to the later years of life: generativity versus stagnation, and ego integrity versus despair. The first, generativity versus stagnation, usually takes place during the mid-adult years; the individual either desires to contribute to future generations or remains stagnant. In the late years of life, individuals will develop a sense of fulfilled life or a sense of despair.

Loss in the Later Years

Loss is one of the most important concepts to understand in the aging process. Losses in the later years are experienced in three major areas: physical, sociological, and emotional.

Within the physical losses of aging there are basically two components: normal aging losses and secondary aging. Normal aging losses include deterioration of the five senses, at different rates for each person. Also involved in normal aging is the loss of muscle strength, the wrinkling of the skin, and the graying of the hair. The second component of physical loss is called secondary aging; and these losses often have disabling effects. Secondary losses include glaucoma and cataracts, which cause visionary impairment; high blood pressure; arterial sclerosis, which affects brain functioning; various types of malignancies; arthritis; bronchitis or emphysema; or kidney problems. These all are chronic illnesses and related to secondary aging. Chronic disorders are common among persons over the age of 65; some suggest that as many as eight older persons out of every ten have a chronic disorder which causes disability. It is important to understand, therefore, that the physical losses of aging have a direct relationship to emotional well-being. A person with cataracts, for example, finds life more limited because of difficulties encountered in reading, driving, walking, and performing routine tasks. No one need be driven into isolation and despair because of physical losses, but these losses do affect behavior in some ways.

There also are losses associated with sociological factors. In the earlier years of life, there are prescribed roles within a culture as child, husband or wife, worker. As one grows old, however, life roles diminish. Males (and, increasingly, females) in old age typically suffer from the loss of the worker role. If one's identity has been linked to the status of the vocation, retirement can bring on mourning over this loss. In the later years alternative roles are limited. Moreover, the goals of older persons may become short-sighted, since they are not encouraged to plan for the future. Finally, sociologically speaking, during the later years of life the social network surrounding the individual seems to constrict and diminish. Friends die, the vocational role is lost, the neighborhood changes—all these are ways in which the associational pattern of existence changes in old age.

Robert Kavanaugh, a former priest and author of *Facing Death,* has outlined seven stages of mourning that an individual experiences when confronting death.[2] These stages may overlap, and persons do not necessarily pass naturally from one stage to the next in sequence.

If aging is seen as an encounter with loss, it might be possible to reinterpret Kavanaugh's categories to gain insight into the existential realities of later life.

Older persons may experience *shock* when the last child leaves home, upon retirement, when income evaporates, or with chronic illness. Widowhood also generates shock. The initial feelings of shock may take the form of denial, since the individual requires protection against what is actually taking place.

Rather than dealing with loss, persons may deny reality. For example, individuals may deny the reality of retirement by putting off planning for it until the last moment. After retirement, persons may still identify with their former occupational status and will often speak of themselves as "former" teachers or insurance salesmen or sales clerks.

Disorientation takes place when older individuals seem unable to cope with experience and have difficulty making decisions. Some forget where they placed objects, or they confuse events. Rather than misinterpreting these reactions as signs of "senility," it may be that they are signs of depression and disorientation over loss. It is important that during this stage persons not be forced to make decisions. Because of confusion, decisions made may not be rational nor in the best interest of the person.

Volatile emotions may mark a new stage of reaction to loss as feelings of injustice over the situation are expressed. A recently retired person may grow angry discussing the former work situation, because he or she feels retirement to be unjust. A parent may express anger in considering children long since gone who do not maintain contact any longer.

Older persons may also feel *guilt* when looking back over their lives. Parents may feel guilty over not spending enough time with their children; spouses may be guilty over actions taken within the marriage.

Loneliness becomes a particularly difficult stage in the later years, as family and friends no longer provide the support required. And there are always reminders of the past.

Regardless of losses experienced, aging can also bring a stage of *relief*. Some persons are relieved when they retire and do not have to face the stress of working. Others find relief in leisure activities, such as painting or reading.

Older persons also may enter a stage of *reestablishment*, in which the present situation is accepted. How does this happen? The answer varies according to the needs and desires of the individual, but the element of self-esteem is crucial. Because persons continue to feel a sense of personal accomplishment and the possibility of making choices about their own lives, new possibilities are opened.

Adaptation in the Later Years

Many persons do adapt successfully to the later years of life and to the losses that are part of the aging process. While it may well be true that persons who in the younger years learned to cope with change adapt more successfully to aging than those who experienced life-adjustment difficulties, there are some other clues for assessing successful aging as well. Persons who age successfully may tend to have one or more of the following personality characteristics:

1. *Awareness of the aging process and acceptance of any limitations imposed as a result of growing old.* Individuals who deny the aging process tend to have difficulty in accepting any limitations involved. An older person, for example, may wish to engage in the same strenuous activities as when he or she was young, but cannot utilize the same skills and strength. Lifelong activities may be maintained into the later years, but with an awareness of the limitations brought about by aging.
2. *Reevaluation of life goals.* Because learning is a lifetime process, successful adaptation is dependent upon the ability to learn from new experiences as one grows old and to make changes in goals. Lifetime goals and interests need not be given up simply because of aging, but there may have to be a reassessment of what is realistically possible.
3. *Search for alternative sources of self-identity and esteem.* For persons whose self-worth is contained within the status derived from an occupational role, the loss of that status in retirement can reduce feelings of personal importance. Those who are able to channel their energies into new pursuits or different roles based on past skills are generally more capable of maintaining self-esteem. Leisure-time activities or volunteer work have traditionally provided this opportunity, but more attention has been paid in the past years to maintenance of employment opportunities, either full- or part-time.

4. *Reinterpretation of the meaning of selfhood.* If the later years bring about a change of status and role, there is an obvious need to reassess the basis for self-evaluation. Work performance or parenthood may no longer provide the opportunity for personal growth, but other alternative resources exist for the continuing growth process. Those who are able to view themselves as having worth apart from any role are usually better equipped to deal with the meaning of selfhood in old age.

Mental Health in the Later Years

Mental health entails a basic sense of self-esteem and power over events. For some older adults, social structures do not promote environments in which ego integrity can be maintained. In the face of losses, despair may arise.

The question of suicide is one that must be considered as part of the problem of despair in the later years. While the suicide rate for women in the United States remains fairly constant as they age, the rate for men increases with age. The suicide rate for American males under the age of 54 is 19.7 per 100,000 population; for women under 54 the rate is 6.8 per 100,000. However, over the age of 55, the suicide rate for men is 39.9 per 100,000; for women the rate is 8.3 per 100,000.[3] The highest suicide rate is among older white males. While each suicide has its own "inner logic," part of the reason for the higher rate among older males may be the loss of status associated with occupational roles, depression over personal problems, or hopelessness associated with some chronic illness.

It is impossible to generalize about the reasons for suicide, for each occupies its own place and time and is connected to a network of other relationships. When it is considered that about 25 percent of all reported suicides involve persons 65 years of age and older, however, there is cause for careful thought. What kind of inner orientation and social environment creates a proclivity toward self-destruction among older adults?

One of the keys to mental health in the later years is that of self-esteem; and a sense of personal worth is rooted in human relationships. It is important, therefore, to be aware of at least three central concerns of older persons in maintaining satisfactory relationships.

1. *Self-concept.* As individuals age, they tend to become more reliant on internal realities and less dependent on external factors. There is a tendency to seek stability within the self, at the very time the self is threatened by outward changes. The self-concept is strengthened by the capacity to find relatedness and stability.
2. *Life review.* Persons in their later years may exhibit a tendency to review their past lives in order to find meaning in the present. This tendency may be mistaken as "rambling" but is in fact a process of reestablishing the self in the light of the aging experience.
3. *Preparation for death.* Older persons are more apt to have experienced the loss of a spouse or friend, simply by virtue of their advanced years. Very often, mourning over losses goes undetected and, for that reason, hampers growth. Creative mourning takes place when individuals are free to grieve and then to move through loss to reestablish relationships with the world.

The Aging Personality

Personality development is a lifelong process. But is there any quality of personal existence which might be said to characterize old age? Are changes in the personality due to bodily losses or to changes in the personal environment or to the ways in which older persons are viewed in a social context?

Studies in the field of personality development in the later years are not at all clear about what specific personality traits can be shown to be due entirely to old age. Some research studies, for example, report finding the aged person as introspective and withdrawing; yet others have found older persons no more likely to withdraw than younger persons—in other words, age could not be seen as a single factor to account for personality development over time. If one argues that aging brings about personality withdrawal, one has not indicated whether the withdrawal is intrinsic to the aging process or conditioned by social forces.

Until future research provides a clearer answer, perhaps it is best to describe various changes in the personality as age-related, but not necessarily caused by aging itself.

Notes

1. Birren, James: "Introduction to the Psychology of Aging," in *Aging: Prospects and Issues,* Richard H. Davis, ed. Los Angeles: Ethel Andrus Gerontology Center, 1973.

2. Kavanaugh, Robert: *Facing Death.* Baltimore: Penguin Books, 1974.

3. Butler, Robert: *Why Survive? Being Old in America.* New York: Harper and Row, 1975, p. 227.

4

The Wisdom of the Body

Bodily Aging

Although individuals may deny their own aging, it is a given reality that with time the body deteriorates. Some theorists argue that it may be possible in the future to slow down the aging process; this would require a new perspective on growing old. Nonetheless, the "wisdom of the body" requires the understanding that bodily organs age at different rates for different individuals.

Physician and gerontologist Merl M. Jackel stresses that all senses are affected as the body grows old. Impaired vision is one indication of aging. Eyesight is usually the first sense to be impaired, beginning in the middle forties. More light is often required to see clearly. Peripheral vision is also adversely affected, which explains why for some older persons crossing a street may be a particularly dangerous activity.

Hearing is also affected with aging. Dr. Jackel claims that the degree and type of hearing deterioration are important. One older individual may have difficulty hearing higher pitches, while low pitches may be the problem for someone else. Individuals also vary in what they hear, which can be referred to as "selective hearing." One older man illustrated this concept in a conversation: "I kept telling my wife to get a hearing aid, but she just wouldn't listen!"

Loss of auditory ability can hasten feelings of isolation among older persons. "Loss of perception of background noises, such as street noises, birds singing, or doors shutting, increases this feeling," Dr. Jackel notes.[1] For this reason, the world without sound becomes "dead." On the positive side, the loss of hearing may enable older persons to work more effectively in the midst of distracting noises.

Sensitivity to pain may also decrease in the later years. This factor can result in difficulties in accurately evaluating ailments. In addition, the sense of equilibrium can be hampered. Such simple activities as changing positions from vertical to horizontal may be difficult for an older person, requiring longer periods of time to regain balance.

Other bodily factors also change with aging. The slower replacement of taste buds leads to a reduction of the sense of taste. The sense of smell is also lessened. As skeletal muscles deteriorate, the body's speed and strength are diminished.

These bodily deteriorations—loss of sight, smell, hearing, strength—are often referred to as *secondary aging.* Nearly 80 percent of persons 65 and over have some chronic disorder, with 35 percent of this number having a chronic disability and 2 percent bedfast. Dr. Jackel lists the following as chronic disorders: cataract and glaucoma; chronic bronchitis and emphysema; arthritis; arterial hypertension; arteriosclerosis affecting either the coronary, cerebral, or kidney arteries; and malignancies of various kinds.[2]

It is important to understand that there is a relationship between the physical and psychological aspects of aging. Physical deterioration can limit such daily activities as dressing, bathing, eating, and shopping. An individual who does not feel adequate physically may also reduce contact with others, out of fear of rejection or embarrassment. For example, there are requirements under most public funding programs to hold public meetings; many times these meetings are held in courthouses or municipal buildings without easy access. Although laws now require that there be public access to such meetings, perhaps through the construction of ramps for wheelchairs, many persons who are physically handicapped feel ill-at-ease in attempting to deal with elevators and other barriers.

Some older adults resent the deterioration of their bodies and may express this resentment verbally or nonverbally—and often to members of their own families. As the body grows old and dependency upon others increases, persons may experience guilt if the situation adversely affects others. If the guilt remains unresolved, persons can retreat into quiet acceptance or outward displays of hostility.

Theories of Aging

Contemporary research does not suggest one universal theory to explain why the body ages; but there are a number of reasons offered to explain the physical aspects of growing old.

Hans Selye, a physician, suggests that there is a close relationship between stress and aging. He writes: "Stress is the sum of all the wear and tear caused by any kind of vital reaction throughout the body at any one time. That is why it can act as a common denominator of all the biologic changes which go on in the body; it is a kind of 'speedometer of life.' "[3]

For the purpose of measuring age, Dr. Selye refers to stress as *physiologic age,* differentiating this from *chronologic age.*[4] Physiologic age is measured by the amount of wear and tear on one's body—not the amount of time that has elapsed since birth. From this perspective, one could agree with Dr. Selye that no one dies of old age; rather persons age and die because one organ wears out and affects the rest of the body. Dr. Selye concludes:

> The lesson seems to be that, as far as man can regulate his life by voluntary actions, he should seek to equalize stress throughout his being, by what we have called *deviation,* the frequent shifting-over of work from one part to the other. The human body . . . wears longest when it wears evenly.[5]

It is important to note that stress need not be viewed as a negative reality. Emotions such as joy and happiness also produce stress, but these can be processes that assist personal well-being.

One theorist, Wilbur Bradbury, argues against the notion that stress is a measure of aging, noting that if wear and tear were the principal causes of aging, the age of death among individuals would vary more than it does. Instead, he proposes a *time-clock theory* of aging:

> As diseases cannot be relied on to kill everyone, the reasoning goes, the human body must be programmed to self-destruct. Nature presumably equips every organism with a time clock set to run down. The timer is called aging; and aging ultimately is death.[6]

The work of Leonard Hayflick tends to support this theory. His research indicates that aging is hastened by faulty or dead cells in the body organs, causing malfunctions. In other words, cells determine their own life expectancy. The fewer the number of times they divide, the nearer the death of the organism.

Another interesting theory might be called the *death-hormone* concept. In this view, "the hormonal system regulates the life span by releasing a 'death hormone' that sabotages the cell."[7] Much research is required on this theory of aging before any firm conclusions can be drawn, but it would be interesting to speculate on whether or not the release of the death-hormone might be brought under control—and thus the aging process delayed.

Whether or not stress is an adequate measure of aging, it is at least an important factor in growing old. How persons cope or do not cope with stress certainly has a relationship to emotional health. On the other hand, if aging and death are programmed, and not open to individual initiative, growing old may be a biochemical process larger than individual life.

There are obviously as many ideas on why people age as there are philosophies of life. Some of these additional ideas are summarized below.

Some researchers believe that there is a relationship between nutrition and aging, noting that the quality and amount of food intake affects the duration of life. Other evidence suggests a correlation between lower temperatures and prolongation of life, while other researchers have concluded that improperly working enzymes assist in the production of defective proteins. Another theory traces its roots to the notion of an immune system in the body, in which various potentially harmful viruses and bacteria are recognized and attacked. As the body ages, it becomes more difficult for healthy and foreign tissues to be distinguished; therefore normal tissue is also attacked. It has also been suggested that thymosin, a hormone that declines as the body ages, may cause the immune system to function ineffectively.

Another medical biologist, Alex Comfort, has sought to simplify what is known about the biology of aging in the following manner. He notes that mammals are made up of three biologic components: cells multiplying or producing newly throughout life (white corpuscles, skin cells); cells that are not capable of division (nerve cells); and noncellular material that may have much or little turnover.[8] Three major theories of aging result from the analysis:

1. Aging takes place through the loss or injury to nonmultiplying cells.
2. Aging takes place when cells change over time.
3. Aging takes place in the inert materials of the body.

There is no final evidence to support any one of the three theories at the expense of the other two. Is aging the result of the loss of cells that cannot be replaced? Do persons age because the new cells produced are not of the same quality as those produced early in life? Or do we age because of changes of colloid, those nonliving parts of the body such as the blood vessel walls or the elastic fibers in them?

Sexuality in the Later Years

Although Sigmund Freud opened up the sexual dimension of human behavior for examination, there remains a myth about aging that stresses the lack of sexual interest and activity in the later years of life. What one means by sexuality also forms the basis for examining sexuality in old age. If sexuality is only conceived of as a genital act, then it may be true that there is a gradual lessening of desire with age. If sexuality is seen in the broader context of touching, embracing, or other physical contact, then sexuality does not diminish with age.

There does appear, however, to be some reduction in sexual desire as the body ages. After menopause, the female's vaginal walls become thinner and sexual intercourse may be painful. Gerontologist Robert Butler suggests that men can lose sexual interest if they lose interest in life. Retirement, for example, if it is viewed as a withdrawal from life, can adversely affect sexual communication.

Researchers at Duke University's Center for the Study of Aging have tentatively suggested the view that rather than decreasing with age, sexuality in some cases increases with age. Over many years of study, it was found that 15 percent of the persons involved showed a steadily increasing rate of sexual interest and activity as they aged.[9] Some physicians urge heart patients to continue sexual activity, believing that this may reduce the possibility of a heart attack, while there is also some evidence to suggest that sexual activity may help to ease the pain of arthritis.

In his book *Existential Sexuality,* philosophy professor Peter Koestenbaum argues that decreased sexual activity in the later years is the result of cultural definitions of beauty. He emphasizes the importance of *choice* in sexuality: choosing one's values and likes and acting upon them, without the onus of cultural definitions. He says that if older people understand this, "they are free to define the meaning of sex; they will be free to set their own standards."[10]

The well-known adage that "beauty is in the eye of the beholder" might well apply to sexuality in the later years. Wrinkles and gray hair need not be unattractive, any more than blond hair and smooth skin should be considered innately sexually attractive. In one of his cases, Koestenbaum had been working with a 69-year-old woman who had had a mastectomy and her 68-year-old husband. At his suggestion, the couple had decided to take a trip abroad to gain some perspective on their situation. Some time later, Koestenbaum received a letter from the wife:

> We were also trying to follow your other suggestion and that was to redefine the meaning of visible physical beauty. Perhaps it is possible for me to believe that Alexander can look at my naked body with one breast drooping like a piece of leather toward the floor and where the other was just a big scar. . . . But at my age it's not worth the trouble. I can do without thinking myself physically gorgeous—I avoid movies and instead read good books. We have beautiful sex between us as it is. I wish you'd tell others how beautiful sex can be at almost seventy.[11]

Because of cultural pressures, it may often appear to those who are older that there is no choice in sexual matters, but the choice remains. Sexuality, much like other life forces, changes with time, and denial of sexuality is only one choice among others for those in their later years.

Health and the Older Individual

Older persons tend to become ill for longer periods of time than younger persons, and thus have a greater need for medical care. It is estimated that 25 percent of the United States' medical costs are accounted for by older persons, although this age group represents approximately 10 percent of the total U.S. population.

While 86 percent (15.4 million persons) of the 65 and over population is estimated to have one or more chronic disorders, most doctors prefer to treat diseases that can be diagnosed and treated more easily, as gerontologist Robert Butler notes. Older persons also have difficulty in receiving medical care when they need it. There are many reasons for this lack of care, but among some of the more prominent are shortage of doctors, inaccessible health care facilities, rising health care costs, and complications resulting from such programs as Medicare and Medicaid. Dr. Butler contends that "because of the rapidly rising costs of health care, the old are actually paying more in dollars than they did before the advent of Medicare some years ago."[12] Medicare, it should be noted, covers less than 50 percent of health care costs and does not cover many of the chronic disorders that represent a significant proportion of health care expenditures.

Medical research may provide ways in the future to eliminate or lessen the impact of chronic disorders, but for the present, emphasis is being placed on preventive health care. From a health maintenance viewpoint, such programs as Medicare are far from adequate since they reach persons only after they have become ill. Title III of the Older Americans Act can be utilized as a source of funding to develop health care maintenance services prior to any illness. Some communities have experimented with the use of hospital clinics in off-hours to provide health monitoring services for older adults. Other communities have equipped vans for mobile health centers, a strategy particularly useful in rural areas.

Nutritional programs, such as those developed under Title VII of the Older Americans Act, can also be a means of preventive health care. Many communities provide the so-called meals-on-wheels program, in which food is actually delivered to the homes of older persons who cannot get out. While home-delivered meals are necessary, critics have argued that such projects can be costly and increase isolation. In response to this type of criticism, Title VII food programs are served in community sites, where large numbers of older persons may come together for a common meal. While donations are accepted, no set charge is permitted for food. The advantage of such programs is that in addition to nutritional services, persons are given opportunities to socialize.

Learning from the Aging Process

Although many older persons do not experience severe limitations on their activities because of health problems, a significant percentage are limited in daily chores because of illness or physical impairment.

The physical aspects of aging are not altogether pleasurable for many of the old. The loss of hearing and diminished sight, less strength and more susceptibility to disease, can be processes difficult to accept. However, just as persons adapt to other realities of aging, so too do they find ways to cope with physical impairments. For example, occupational therapists are able to equip living quarters to meet the needs of physically handicapped older adults so that there is little interruption of daily activities. Learning to adjust to the aging body where required is a step toward continued growth in the latter years of life.

Notes

1. Jackel, Merl M.: "Senescence," in *Personality Development and Deviation,* George H. Wiedeman, ed. New York: International Universities Press, 1975, p. 433.

2. Ibid., p. 434.

3. Selye, Hans: *The Stress of Life.* New York: McGraw-Hill, 1956, p. 274.

4. Ibid., p. 274.

5. Ibid., p. 276.

6. Bradbury, Wilbur: *The Adult Years.* New York: Time-Life Books, 1975, pp. 137–140.

7. Ibid., p. 140.

8. Comfort, Alex: *The Process of Aging.* New York: The New American Library, 1964, pp. 97–98.

9. Galton, Lawrence: *Don't Give up on an Aging Parent.* New York: Crown Publishers, 1975, p. 172.

10. Koestenbaum, Peter: *Existential Sexuality.* Englewood Cliffs, N.J.: Prentice-Hall, 1974, p. 101.

11. Ibid., p. 104.

12. Butler, Robert N.: *Why Survive? Being Old in America.* New York: Harper and Row, 1975, p. 209.

5

Social Values and the Aging Process

A Brief History of Social Gerontology

Social gerontology is a relatively new field of study and is only beginning to attract serious scholarly interest. As the percentage of the population over the age of 60 increases, so too will the necessity of establishing gerontology as a distinct discipline, with roots and linkages within other branches of the social and physical sciences.

What is social gerontology? Gerontologist Robert C. Atchley writes: "The sociological aspect of aging deals with the society in which aging occurs, the influence this society has on the aging individual, and the influence he has on it."[1] From this vantage point it can be seen that social gerontology is concerned, not only with society, but also with the responses of the individual to that society. Clark Tibbitts, one of the fathers of social gerontology, also described this new discipline in a similar way, identifying both the individual and the society as subjects for gerontological study.

It was not until the late 1940s that social gerontology began to become a field for serious research and debate. In fact, Tibbitts noted in the lead article of the first issue of the *Journal of Gerontology* in 1946 that he was unable to find any significant amount of social science research in aging, or any semblance of any organized field of study.[2] However, another early gerontologist, Robert J. Havighurst, traces the roots of social gerontology to the establishment of "old people's homes" in Europe several centuries ago, and says that by the end of the 19th century it was becoming obvious that as a result of industrialization there was a loss of role and status among elderly family members. But, Havighurst argues, the first stage of social gerontological emphasis took place around 1900, when various countries worked out old-age pension systems. The second stage of development took place when older members of families could no longer afford to remain in their own homes, and there was a need for public and private housing for them. Finally, the third stage of development was evident when there was a movement to look beyond the material comforts of older persons to their need for ego support—toward having a function and purpose in society. In some respects, this third stage is still with us today.

Tibbitts argues that one of the early difficulties in establishing gerontology as a distinct science rested with the confusion about what it means to be old. The onset of aging was seen as an arbitrary process, due in part to two sometimes conflicting concepts: the social definition of aging, and the physical processes of aging. For example, the societal definition of "old age" might list retirement as the signal for growing old, usually around the age of 65. However, not every individual who reaches the age of 65 is old in a psychological sense; and for many women who have lived more traditional roles of spouse and mother, retirement does not occur at any age.

Atchley prefers to discuss the concept of "advanced adulthood" in three stages, rather than utilizing a chronological definition of aging. He lists the three stages as: Middle Age (usually between the ages of 40 and 60), Later Maturity (between the ages of 60 and 80), and Old Age (after the age of 80). Another way to view these stages might be: Middle Age (between the ages of 40 and 60), the Young Old (generally between the ages of 60 and 80), and the Old Old (80 and over). Individuals, however, cannot be neatly placed within any one category, since they may combine characteristics of many stages at the same time. Some theorists, for example, believe that those within the category of Young Old think of themselves as middle-aged, not as elderly, and therefore tend to have more in common with the values and life-styles of that period of life rather than with those of old age.

The Social Situation

Sociologists tend to approach the study of aging from two perspectives: macro- and microlevel analysis. At the macrolevel sociologists study large aggregates of persons, of nations, and of social organizations. The intent is to understand the larger social order in which aging takes place. At the microlevel study is directed toward understanding changes in an individual's world through the passage of time.

At the macrolevel most Western countries are in the midst of a population shift that is revolutionary in scope and presents the picture of a changed social order. Some have termed this phenomenon the "geriatric revolution." There are currently about 23 million Americans over the age of 65; by the turn of the century about 31 million persons will be 65 or over. Somewhere in the early part of the 21st century it is projected that 50 million individuals will be past their 65th birthday. By the year 2040, all age groups will be equally represented in the population; the median age of the population will be 40, as compared to 28 in 1970. A decrease in infant mortality rates and better health care for all age groups contributes in part to this population shift, but equally significant is the fact that women are bearing fewer children per family unit.

The geriatric revolution will have sweeping effects on all age groups and will be particularly difficult in countries that have tended to glorify youthfulness, progress, and change. For one thing, national policies will need to be changed to respond to the needs of older persons; some argue that, as part of the developing needs, there will have to be dramatic changes in pension plans and distribution of income. Employment practices may also gradually change to permit older persons to continue working as they desire, rather than forcing retirement at a certain age. Already, the U.S. Congress has challenged the wisdom of such a shift in mandatory retirement policies.

Not all social theorists are optimistic about the national will and ability to provide for the changes required. Some advance the theory that the older population itself will resist the very changes needed; they believe, in addition, that there may be a movement backward in time: to local control of communities, traditional family structures, and more conventional social mores.

Whatever the case, if the present population trends continue, a new set of individual and social relationships will be engendered. Taking the contrary argument from those who feel that an aging culture may be more rooted in tradition, and therefore more conservative, it might also be argued that in the future the source of social change may originate within the older adult population. Older persons already tend to be the heaviest voting bloc in the population; as their numbers increase, so too will their influence. Ironically, it has been thought that young people represent the unsettling element in the culture; in the future, the shakers may be those in the later years of life.

Reorganizers and Disorganizers

The later years may be a time of creativity and vitality. Studies of older persons conclude that old age is generally marked by self-esteem and positive morale. One 76-year-old individual symbolized this successful adjustment to old age when he remarked, "These are the greatest years of my life. For the first time I can be myself without having to worry about what others think." This person represents what has been called a *reorganizer*: a person who adapts to retirement by substituting new activities for the past vocational role. In the early or middle years, many persons feel as if they cannot make free choices, because of the pressures of family or income. In the later years, however, many find time to pursue previously unrealized goals. Reorganizers are persons who adapt to the late years of life with self-esteem and relatively high morale. Of course, it can be argued that those older persons who are reorganizers displayed this attitude throughout their lives.

Disorganizers are persons who in the later years do not remain involved in life; often apathy and despair set in. In many cases their perceptions are a carryover from attitudes held throughout life; growing old simply increases the sense of futility. Part of this feeling may be rooted in biochemical origins; aging does bring about various bodily changes, which may result in economic difficulties and lingering health problems. But the social environment in which persons age often adversely affects self-image; the loss of income and role status in particular hamper continued involvement.

Some Major Theories in Social Gerontology

Since social gerontology is a relatively new development in the social sciences, and its theoretical base is still being formulated, philosophies of aging are still in their infancy. Three theories of aging appear to warrant consideration, however.

The *disengagement theory* holds that as a person ages, he or she tends to reduce the number of interpersonal relationships and alter the quality of those remaining. Society must provide a way for an orderly transition of power from the old to the young, while also preparing the old to die. Mandatory retirement is one way this disengagement is structured in society. But there also is a gradual process involving a series of role losses (worker, parent) which triggers disengagement. At the same time that society promotes disengagement, moreover, the individual disengages, withdrawing from life and becoming more self-occupied, until death (the final disengagement).

Elaine Cumming and William E. Henry first proposed the disengagement theory in their 1961 book, *Growing Old: The Process of Disengagement.* They wrote:

> Disengagement is an inevitable process in which many of the relationships between a person and other members of society are severed, and those remaining are altered in quality.[3]

Cumming and Henry later refined their original theory, but their thrust seems to be that social involvement decreases with age —and this is done to fulfill a function within society. Later social research, however, has only conditionally supported this theory, and in some cases the theory has been refuted. For example, other studies have shown that where old persons are in relatively good health and have adequate income, social disengagement does not take place on a major scale.

The *activity theory,* on the other hand, states that the norms for old age are the same as those for middle age, and that often older people will deny their age for as long as possible. In this view, activity is seen as a path leading toward adjustment or life satisfaction; older persons do not withdraw from society but rather become more involved if circumstances permit. Yet this theory fails to account for significant numbers of older persons who do not cope. Activity, in other words, does not always lead to meaning, prompting some critics in the field to comment that older adult activity centers are nothing more than "playpens for the elderly."

The *life-cycle theory* sets up a period of an individual's life known as old age and holds that this stage of life is distinct from others. As mentioned previously, Erik Erickson developed such a concept and categorized old age as a struggle between ego identity and despair. Bernice Neugarten also argues for such a designation, and writes: "with increasing old age, ego functions are turned inward. . . . There is also a movement of energy away from an outer-world to an inner-world orientation."[4]

Some other observations about aging also require attention. Irving Rosow, a social theorist, argues that individuals are not effectively socialized to old age, unlike other life stages. He finds nine cycles in an individual's life: infancy, childhood, adolescence, young adulthood, marriage, parenthood, middle age, grandparenthood, and old age. Rosow believes that there are role transitions between each of these nine cycles, rites of passage into the next—with the exception of passage into old age. For example, a marriage ceremony serves as a rite of passage into being married, as the birth of the first child signifies parenthood. In most cases, moreover, the individual moves from a position of lower to higher status, and there are means provided to do so smoothly.

Yet in studying the passage into old age, Rosow notes: "An old person's life is basically 'roleless,' unstructured by the society, and conspicuously lacking in norms."[5] In passing into old age there are few clear rites of passage. Retirement might be considered one rite of passage, particularly for men who have worked all their lives, while widowhood might signal a rite of passage for older women. Often, institutionalization may signal passage into old age for others. Rosow believes that passage into old age signifies loss of status; moreover, the passage is not smooth and there is role confusion.

Sociologist Arnold M. Rose suggests that an aging subculture is developing; he defines a subculture as a group that interacts more with its own members than with other segments of society. "The elderly," he writes, "tend to interact with each other increasingly as they get older, and with younger persons decreasingly, and hence develop a subculture."[6]

Rose claims that older persons are on their way to becoming a voting bloc, and with increasing age consciousness will exercise significant impact on society at large. The difficulty with this view, however, is that data on the political values of older persons do not tend to support the thesis of a cohesive voting bloc; on the contrary, the political values of older adults remain diversified.

Roles in the Later Years

A role is based on three essential factors: (1) what is expected of a person in a given position; (2) what people do in a given position; (3) what a particular person does in a given position.[7]

In most industrial societies, older persons generally occupy lower roles in the social system in terms of status; this has prompted some gerontologists to believe that aging is primarily a study of the loss of roles among older people. *The Kansas City Study of Adult Life,* which consists of interviews with 168 older persons over a five-year period, reached a contrary conclusion, however. This study cast doubt on the disengagement theory of aging. According to the researchers who conducted the study: "We believe . . . that the majority of people in the dominant American culture who are age fifty and over will be found to be relatively successful agers."[8]

What are some role changes in later life? Retirement obviously signals the beginning of a new role. Retirement need not be seen entirely in a negative way, although mandatory retirement is an issue that consistently troubles older-adult organizations. However, there appears to be no cohesive retirement role; decisions about what to do with new leisure time are left to the individual. Generally, it has been found that those who best adapted to past challenges in life cope most easily with retirement. Although women are now entering the world of work outside the home, most within the present generation did not hold full-time jobs. The retirement of their spouses, therefore, also signals a new period of adjustment for older women. Once again, clearly defined roles for the older woman who no longer takes care of a husband and children are limited.

Grandparenthood is one major role for the older adult. The federal Foster Grandparent Program seeks to develop this role by reimbursing older adults for volunteer work as "grandparents" in such areas as day care centers and schools. The existence of such a program also points to the need for "grandparents" in a highly mobile society.

The death of a spouse brings about a new role for many older persons—more often women than men since on the average women outlive their husbands. Widowhood is a significant role designation for many of the old.

New Roles in the Future of Aging

In the future new alternative roles will be required for older adults, beyond the more traditional roles of grandparent or volunteer worker. The difficulty of role selection currently is that the potential range of choice is extremely limited, without social sanctions and support systems for new roles. Some potentially new roles for aging persons in the future are suggested below.

1. Second careers. Just as many workers have the opportunity to be retrained for new or expanding occupations, so too should older persons be provided with the chance to engage in studies leading to new careers. The responsibility for such programs might best be given to educational institutions; many colleges and universities are already developing such possibilities. Within each community, there are service positions that do not require a normal work-week and that are frequently not filled by younger workers. For example, with some basic training, older persons without prior experience might assume part-time positions as library workers, municipal government assistants, or social service workers. At the same time, colleges and universities providing such second-career training might consider using older persons as trainers and instructors.

2. Consultation. Especially in other cultures, older adults are frequently consulted about problems facing a family, organization, or community. Although efforts have been made in the United States on a small scale to develop a pool of retired persons as consultants (the Small Business Administration uses the skills of retired persons with business skills to consult with small and developing industries and companies), little has been done to promote such a venture on a massive scale nationally. A national consulting service, perhaps funded by the federal government and private business, might well provide a means of utilizing the lifetime talents of older persons for projects that benefit entire communities.

3. Employment. The relaxation of mandatory retirement laws should provide an opportunity for those older persons who desire to continue working to do so. However, public employment programs, such as those funded under the federal Comprehensive Employment and Training Act, should respond to the need for jobs for older adults. New categories of positions, such as public homemaker services for older adults, should also be considered.

Culture and Aging

Aging is a cultural as well as psychological and biological process. Traditionally there have been two cultural measures of aging: (1) *functional*: the end of active adult status, usually measured by biological deterioration; (2) *formal*: a change of status linked to some symbolic event. In Western culture the formal definition of age is most frequently employed and is often associated with chronological time.

Margaret Clark and Barbara Gallatin conducted a study of 435 older persons in San Francisco in order to develop a cultural framework for understanding the aging process. Their study looked at the personal and social realities of aging.

At the level of individual aging, the researchers found that only a small percentage of those studied viewed aging negatively, nor was there much difference between age groups. Lower estimates of aging, however, tended to be linked to mental and physical status, with morale decreasing for those in the lower economic groups. The researchers conclude:

> Life after sixty shares with adolescence an intensification of the intimate and self-reflexive. . . . Both are times of mental and physical metamorphosis, as both adolescent and elder become absorbed in the workings of their own bodies and minds, watching these internal changes with a mingling of wonder and dismay. Then, too, a kind of loneliness or increasing sense of privacy grows as a natural consequence from this self-absorption.[9]

The older individual also held various personal goals; among these were independence, social acceptability, adequacy of personal resources, and ability to cope with both external threats and changes in the self. The researchers discovered eight sources of low morale: dependency, physical discomfort or sensory loss, loneliness, boredom, mental discomfort, loss of prestige, fear of dying, and problems of others.

While Clark and Gallatin found few data to support the theory of disengagement, they did report a somewhat negative picture of how society structures the aging process:

> Old age . . . is a time of dramatic change in one's social . . . significance. Whole sets of statuses may be lost, or to all intents and purposes, become non-functional within the short space of a few years. Children grow up, marry, and leave home. Forced retirement may ease a man out of his worker status. The chances of widowhood increase. And our culture provides almost no statuses to replace these. . . . Our data lead us to believe that most of the old people we interviewed were not at all happy to rest content with the "inescapable fact" of growing old.[10]

A Double-Bind Theory of Aging

Many social theories have been advanced regarding aging, but at times they appear to contradict each other. Part of this conflict could, perhaps, be traced to the newness of the field itself; however, it is possible that the contradictions are contained in the reality being defined—that, in fact, aging in contemporary culture is a paradox rather than a unified subject. Such a position forms the basis for what will be called the *double-bind theory of aging.*

A double-bind is a situation in which a person is given alternative choices of behavior, none of which leads to positive results. For example, a father may say to his son, "Come here, son, I want to talk to you," but his voice may be stern and angry. The son is caught by the contradiction; he has been asked to come, but knows that whether he does so or not the father still will be angry. The double-bind theory has been described in work among terminally ill patients, when doctors may verbalize to a patient that he is progressing but communicate hopelessness. It may also be possible to apply this concept to the entire aging process, at least as it reveals itself in modern society.

The most obvious cultural double-bind in aging relates to a dominant American value: independence. Throughout life, individuals are told to seek freedom; freedom is independence, and only by being independent can a person find respect and esteem. Yet, with regard to older persons, after the age of 65, culture sets up environments of dependence. The older person is denied access to social wealth and to societal involvement. On the one hand, social policy is directed toward promoting independence among older persons (the major thrust of the Federal Older Americans Act is to promote independent living); yet the social environment promotes dependence, while all the time conditioning persons to fear becoming dependent.

Another major cultural double-bind is in the area of productivity. The dominant culture places a premium on work, yet at the same time forces older persons to retire. Under this pervasive value structure, it is somewhat senseless to argue that older persons should find other outlets in retirement to compensate for loss of the vocational role. The fact is that this culture ascribes worth to a person's job role, and retirement does not bear a positive connotation. The entire area of "senior centers" is a weak attempt to develop alternatives to the double-bind; but as long as older persons are systematically denied access to work, these attempts will have only secondary impact.

The dominant value placed on the family—particularly marriage and couplehood—produces still another double-bind situation at the time of the death of a spouse. This dilemma most frequently confronts older women who have placed a high value on marriage only to discover widowhood at the end. The cultural message regarding self-identity in the later years is that experience brings on responsibility and a reasonable disinterestedness. Yet many older persons facing death are in fact facing totally new personal and societal situations that call for new behavior. Few societal patterns provide ways to cope with difficult situations that are distinct from their earlier years.

The double-bind theory points out the conflicts of the later years and illustrates why it is difficult to arrive at a single, unified view of growing old. The theory focuses not only on what is supposed to be, but also on what is—and therein lies the difficulty of growing old in the modern world.

It is no wonder, then, that some of the more radical theorists point out that it will be impossible to improve the environment of aging in modern industrialized societies until the entire social order is changed. Some argue that the social environment of the elderly is a clear symbol of the hypocrisy of the total social system. They feel that only after a revolution in thinking—in reordering the world of work and leisure, family and community, social policy and programs—can there be a lasting, positive impact on the fastest growing age group in America.

Social Change and Social Policy

Can social change result in an environment for the older person which provides the opportunity for continued growth? The evidence is still somewhat mixed. Some theorists, such as Arnold Rose, believe that aging persons represent an emerging subculture that is on its way to becoming a powerful force for change. Rose agrees with the argument that as the number of older persons in society increases, social policy will be required to speak to their needs. The Gray Panthers, therefore, as a politically active group seeking to raise consciousness about growing old, could have a decided impact on social change.

Certainly there appears to be a growing awareness of the concerns of older persons in recent years, but Rosow takes a less hopeful look at social change through organized efforts on their behalf. He believes that older persons will not organize themselves around single issues without difficulty, and in fact are a heterogeneous group within the general population. While there may have been some gains in the provision of services to older adults, these gains take place at a slower rate than is needed.

The type of social change involved is perhaps the key in looking toward the future. The civil rights movement in its earlier days emphasized integration into the mainstream of society as a vehicle for change. Rosow sees little hope of such integration taking place between older citizens and the rest of society. Another avenue of change, however, seeks not so much to integrate a group into the mainstream of culture, but to assure its independence and integrity. In a manner similar to that of the civil rights movement after the days of integration, older adults may first find it necessary to increase awareness of what it means to be old within their own age group before seeking full entrance into the wider community.

Notes

1. Atchley, Robert C.: *The Social Forces in Later Life.* Belmont, Calif.: Wadsworth Publishing, 1972, p. 5.

2. Vedder, Clyde B.: *Gerontology: A Book of Readings.* Springfield, Ill.: Charles C. Thomas, 1963, p. 7.

3. Cumming, Elaine, and Henry, William E.: *Growing Old: The Process of Disengagement.* New York: Basic Books, 1961, p. 211.

4. Neugarten, Bernice L. (ed.): *Middle Age and Aging.* Chicago: University of Chicago Press, 1972, p. 140.

5. Rosow, Irving: *Socialization to Old Age.* Berkeley: University of California Press, 1974, pp. 68–69.

6. Neugarten, Bernice L. (ed.): *Middle Age and Aging.* Chicago: University of Chicago Press, 1972, p. 29.

7. Atchley, Robert C.: *The Social Forces in Later Life.* Belmont, Calif.: Wadsworth Publishing, 1972, p. 99.

8. Williams, Richard H., and Wirths, Claudine G.: *Lives through the Years.* New York: Atherton Press, 1965, p. 211.

9. Clark, Margaret, and Gallatin, Barbara: *Culture and Aging.* Springfield, Ill.: Charles C. Thomas, 1967, p. 78.

10. Ibid., pp. 134–135.

6

Public Policies and the Older Person

Cultural Values and Public Policy

Public policies related to older persons reflect prevailing cultural values. It is important, however, that a clear distinction be made between those values in which a culture professes belief and those values that are actually operating in social relationships. At times these two views can exist harmoniously, but with regard to the situation of older persons in modern America there appears to be a conflict between stated values of aging and the status of the aged.

As has been shown previously, American culture proclaims independence as a primary value, tracing its roots to pre-Revolutionary times. Individuals are supposed to be protected in their independence against the impositions of government; above all else, the dominant values appear to stress individual freedom against institutional demands. Nonetheless, the values underneath those expressed as central betray another set of beliefs, which are reinforced by public policy. These values tend to support those policies which have as their unwritten objective dependence upon social systems. The explosion of social services to the aged, particularly evident in the Social Security system, create environments of dependency rather than self-sufficiency. If the values of the culture truly supported independence, there would be no requirement for these federal and state programs.

Public policy in the field of aging suffers from cultural lag; the policies developed over the past 40 years since the beginnings of Social Security seem to be directed toward meeting only minimum needs. Rather than anticipating social problems, policies react only to those current issues of immediate concern.

In spite of programs directed toward older persons in America, there is no viable national policy on aging. Instead, policies move from crisis to crisis in order to patch up a damaged system.

Some Policy Issues in Aging

Public policy is basically an attempt to provide a rational framework for the development of social systems in order to reach desirable goals. Much of what is thought to be new policy and planning goals in actuality consists of variations on the social philosophy of the 19th-century writer John Stuart Mill, an exponent of *utilitarianism.* The basic theses of utilitarian thought were: (1) policy is to be directed toward the promotion of the greatest happiness of the greatest number of persons in any given society; (2) social programs are to be assessed in terms of their results, and these results are judged as right in proportion to the amount and kind of happiness produced; (3) policy should be guided by an awareness of which consequences tend to promote the greatest good for the greatest number of individuals. The contemporary management-by-objectives approach, often used as a method for developing social programs, is an outgrowth of utilitarian philosophy.

The management-by-objectives (MBO) approach seeks to clarify social goals so that results can be measured. For example, social planners might specify a goal of providing transportation to older persons in the following statement: "The objective will be to provide 3000 persons 60 years of age and older in the region with community transit services that operate five days a week and provide door-to-door service." Here, the outcome of policy—transportation for older persons—has been clarified, and the intended results specified in terms of actual numbers. The emphasis on those results that tend to produce the greatest good for the greatest number is utilitarian.

Although policy development is dependent upon cultural attitudes and made more complex by the unintended ways in which policy is implemented, there are three basic questions concerning policy issues in aging which require examination:

1. Do older people actually require help? In spite of the fact that a significant percentage of the older adult population lives in poverty or near-poverty conditions, the response to this first policy question determines the shape of future programs. There are those who believe that a policy of "benign neglect" should rule all decisions, since any increase in public or private services to older persons simply increases the likelihood of dependence, a factor contrary to the expressed need of independence. If any programs develop as a result of this policy orientation, most should be directed toward increasing the income of older citizens or supporting self-help projects, both of which enable persons to remain independent. Proponents of this view argue that older persons themselves resist intervention, particularly those connected to public welfare activities. While some admit that often an activistic interpretation of policy may create further administrative nightmares and dependency, others argue that the existence of significant proportions of the aged population in the low-income bracket demands a response, and that the traditional helpers of society—families, communities, and churches—no longer adequately fulfill that function.

2. *Do older persons actually want help?* Even if policy makers agree that there is a need and desire for services, there remains the question of whether older persons actually desire such assistance. The response to this policy issue rests with a definition of what is meant by help. If assistance is seen in a patronizing way—What can we do to help you?—then persons who have been removed from decision making will tend to resent any assistance. Perhaps a less paternalistic way of phrasing the same question that would yield more participatory results would be: How can older persons help themselves, and other persons as well?

3. *Can anything really be done anyway?* The response to this issue need not imply a pervasive pessimism, but a realization that policy decisions may create as many problems as are solved. Some theorists have argued that many of the more difficult issues facing persons are the result of past efforts to solve particular problems. The difficulty with this view is not with its sense of hopelessness, but rather with its departure from reality. For better or worse, services to older adults are multiplying across the nation, so that something already is being done. The issue is whether the activities being carried out for older persons are effective and efficient and address their real needs.

The Older Americans Act

The Older Americans Act of 1965 was the most comprehensive move made to that time toward a national policy on aging, providing grants to states and local communities to address the issues of older adults.

Until 1973 states acted as the clearinghouse for grants under the Act and provided funds for community projects. During 1965 and 1973 many programs were initiated, but those operated most frequently through senior centers. The 1973 amendments to the Act changed the focus of the program from a series of projects under a state governmental office to a system of operation based in regional offices on aging (usually called Area Agencies on Aging). The structural changes that took place as a result of the 1973 amendments varied from state to state. Some states, such as Rhode Island, retained a single planning and service agency for the entire area; but most frequently state offices were decentralized so that in each region of the state there were offices on aging. Area Agencies on Aging themselves also followed different organizational models. Pennsylvania, for example, with a county system of government, placed its area agency operations within the county structure, while other states, such as Massachusetts and Connecticut, found it necessary to develop nonprofit corporations outside the governmental structure to act as area agencies. Both service-delivery models had strengths and weaknesses. From within a governmental unit, aging organizations could avail themselves of other federal and state funds and maintain a close liaison with elected officials. At the same time, however, the organizations were subject to the political influence of elected officials. For those organizations in the nonprofit sector, such political interference was less, but often at the cost of being kept on the outside of the political decision-making process.

The Older Americans Act is made up of a number of sections, which speak to specific areas of activity. However, a series of ten national objectives formed the basis for future policy; each of these objectives was stated in terms of older Americans and included the following "bill of rights" for the aged:

1. An adequate income in retirement
2. The best possible mental and physical health
3. Suitable housing, designed with reference to the special needs of the older adult population
4. Full restorative services for those who require institutionalization
5. Opportunity for employment
6. Retirement opportunities
7. Pursuit of meaningful leisure-time activities
8. Efficient community services

9. Immediate benefit from proven research
10. Freedom and independence

In order to begin meeting these national objectives, the Act was divided into various sections, or titles, to promote community services. The major titles of the Act, and a brief description of each section, are included here.

Title III. This section provides for a broad range of community service programs, usually administered by state offices on aging and a network of Area Agencies on Aging. The Act requires older-adult participation in planning and developing programs (the usual requirement is that 51 percent of advisory councils be composed of persons 60 years of age and older). Typical projects funded under this title include: transportation, home repair services, health, and information and referral. Agencies using Title III funds are usually given decreasing funds each year and are urged to develop other sources of revenue to support programs.

Title IV. This section provides for research and training opportunities in the field of aging. Part A provides funds for training, with an emphasis on activities taking place at colleges and universities. Part B funds research projects. Part C includes money for the establishment of multidisciplinary gerontology centers, where various research and training projects are developed.

Title V. This section establishes funding for the renovation and development of senior centers.

Title VII. This section provides for a national nutrition program for persons 60 years of age and older; although smaller percentages of these funds may be used for meals-on-wheels programs, the larger share is set aside for group, or congregate, feeding projects. Agencies using these funds are required to provide other social services (such as legal services or consumer education) at their feeding sites. No set fees can be established for the cost of meals, although voluntary contributions are accepted.

Title IX. This section provides for part-time employment opportunities for persons age 60 and over.

In order to receive funds under the Older Americans Act, each state must prepare an annual plan and hold a series of public hearings. Area Agencies, in turn, submit regional plans to the state for funding.

At its best, the Act creates a new network of organizations across the country active in the issues of aging, and a consequent flurry of new projects. At its worst, unrealistic expectations are created by these new projects. In 1978, the Older Americans Act was renewed for three years; this resulted in a number of major changes:

1. Titles III, V, and VII were consolidated into one service program.
2. Area Agencies on Aging were required to develop three-year plans for services.
3. In each region, at least 50 percent of Title III funding must be spent on either access services (transportation, outreach) or legal services.
4. Statewide programs to reach residents of nursing homes were mandated.
5. Little or no increase in funding appeared likely, although there were requirements for new or expanded services.

The Government Maze

A broad and often confusing array of federal, state, and local policies have impact on the lives of older persons. Often these policies conflict, as was the case with many elderly residents of public housing when Social Security rates were increased, placing them in higher income brackets and thereby subject to additional rent charges.

It is difficult enough for the trained eye to identify the agencies serving older persons and practically impossible for the older consumer to do so without quite an effort. It has been estimated, for example, that there are approximately 92,000 tax-levying governments in the country,[1] many of which also provide various services.

Major governmental support of older persons came with the passage of the Social Security Act in the United States in the 1930s, which was intended to provide partial financial support to those in the retirement years. In the United States in 1970, over 85 percent of the population age 65 and over were receiving Social Security benefits. It would be impossible within the scope of this book to summarize the full details of the Social Security system. In 1974 it took the U.S. Department of Health, Education and Welfare 504 pages to develop a Social Security Handbook listing purposes and requirements of the Act.

While Social Security amounts to about 34 percent of the total aggregate income of retirees, the average monthly amount paid a couple in 1973 was $270. It must be remembered, however, that although this amount seems meager to support a couple for a month, the original intent of the law was to provide only *partial* replacement for earnings lost through retirement. In 1945, there were 35 wage earners to every Social Security recipient; today there are about three wage earners to every recipient, meaning that income to support the system does not keep pace with payments.

Disjointed Incrementalism

One of the leading students of policy making, economist Charles E. Lindblom, has outlined a theory of "disjointed incrementalism" for explaining how most policy is developed. According to this view, policy makers do not deal with great issues one at a time, but instead reach decisions on a piecemeal basis for particular problems. This view differs from the comprehensive notion of policy making, which classically postulates persons choosing from among a broad range of alternatives, carefully weighing the costs and benefits, and then selecting a course of action. Lindblom argues that man is too limited for this comprehensive model:

> The piecemealing, remedial incrementalist or satisficer may not look like a heroic figure. He is nevertheless a shrewd, resourceful problem-solver who is wrestling bravely with a universe that he is wise enough to know is too big for him.[2]

Notes

1. Jones, Charles O.: *An Introduction to the Study of Public Administration.* Belmont, Calif.: Duxbury Press, 1970, p. 6.

2. Lindblom, Charles E.: *The Policy-Making Process.* Englewood Cliffs, N.J.: Prentice-Hall, 1968, p. 27.

7

Planning Programs for Older Adults

The Case for Planning in Aging

Whenever an individual or a group of persons set intentional goals, a planning process has been set in motion. The common complaint often registered against planning is directed at the technology of planning—the collection of information and research studies, computers, and sophisticated charts—with the negative reaction that planners do little more than gather statistics in reports, which in turn gather dust in libraries. More than one citizen has complained to public officials of planning reports that show little promise of yielding any positive solution. "What I want to see is a little action," someone inevitably says. The argument against the compilation of information for its own sake is well-taken. Yet the implication of action without planning is equally alarming. Planning presupposes some measure of rationality required to reach goals; rather than have persons become victims of events, planning implies that somewhere in the process human intervention can change the course of events.

Planning in the field of aging is of recent vintage, although persons have of course developed plans for older adults in the past. More frequently, past planning had centered on physical projects, such as the building of a nursing home or the construction of housing. It has not been that long ago since physical and human planning in the social environment have come to be seen as necessary components in a total process. And it was only recently that planners in the field of aging began to develop comprehensive systems involving not only older persons, but also their relationship to the entire community. Whether a person works as a counselor or nurse among older patients or as a professional planner who must deal with community systems, the element of planning is essential. The counselor, for example, must have some goals in mind for the patient and, like the nurse, must have some method of assessing the patient's progress.

Planning Problems in Aging

The systematic development of planning in the field of aging is still in its infancy. Only recently, with the passage of the Older Americans Act, was a comprehensive planning mechanism envisioned that could tap public and private resources while seeking to link up a wide range of community programs. One of the reasons planners neglected the field of aging can be traced to the general feeling of unimportance that was attached to older persons themselves. Other community issues, such as transportation or employment, were felt to be more urgent. In addition, older persons often appeared powerless. Until recently, other interest groups waged struggles to gain the attention of policy makers, and the older citizens seemed relatively quiet and stable.

The demand for planning and for new programs in the field of aging has come as much from organized efforts among older persons as from those in positions of authority. The strength in terms of eligible voters has become evident among older adults. For example, about 15 percent of eligible voters are older persons, and approximately 65 percent of this number vote regularly. In the 1974 Congressional elections, 63 million Americans cast ballots, of which 22 million were 55 years of age or older. The question has been whether this older segment of the population could organize itself as a powerful lobbying force, overcoming economic and geographical differences. Such groups as the Gray Panthers seek to form coalitions to promote the causes of older persons; but there are political theorists who believe that such efforts will result in a backlash from among younger segments of the population.

Public and private responses to the needs of any special group usually take place only after a problem has become so severe that action is demanded, or until those who are particularly adversely affected require attention. In this view, planners always appear to be playing a catch-up game, and seldom with adequate resources.

Another difficulty in developing comprehensive plans for older adults is the parochialism evident at most levels of government.

While there are obvious differences between the status of older persons in rural Alabama and in the urban centers of the Northeast, there are also some common areas of need: transportation, income maintenance, health care. Unfortunately, the needs are seldom addressed systematically. Local communities desire local control and often resent intervention by state or federal government. At the same time, federal and state efforts are often fragmented.

At the planning level there are often two, apparently conflicting, philosophies involved. The first philosophy begins with the assumption that individuals can best solve their problems on their own, without the interference of planners. The other philosophy begins with a different assumption: that rational, systematic action is required. Somewhere in between these two philosophies is a middle position, which seems most frequently advocated. The view here is that what is required is a rational means of assessing needs, developing and coordinating resources, providing services to meet needs on a priority basis, involving older persons in determining their own projects, and assessing the results.

General Planning Principles

What is planning? First, planning is the attempt to attain certain goals within a community. In a more centralized social order, planning may be directly related to the achievement of those plans, so that the act of developing plans has an orderly infusion into the lives of citizens. In democratic societies, planners are called upon to become advisors to those who make public policy decisions; systems of accountability to those who live within the community are supposed to be developed.

Second, planning is intended to be a rational process. This assumption is based on the belief that social change requires intentional action—that is, that rather than leaving community development in the hands of chance or at the mercy of those with political power, decision making that is based on rational goals must be brought into play.

Of central concern to the question of planning is the nature of community goal selection and development. Planners do not work in isolation from the people they serve, although many might wish to believe their art could be made more effective without participation from the community. Sociologist and planner Herbert J. Gans argues, however, that planners and other professionals do not monopolize knowledge about the goals and values of the community. "Diversity is valuable," he writes, "and people are entitled to live in any way they choose, unless that way can be proved to be destructive to them or their fellow men."[1]

Gans is a proponent of what he calls *goal-oriented planning.* This planning approach begins with the assumption that each community retains certain desirable goals for itself; the task of the planner is then to assist the community in clarifying those goals and placing them in some order of priority.

Because resources often are limited and goals unrealistic, planners must also be able to help communities select priorities. "The most important role of the planner is, however, to tell the community and its leaders that if they want to achieve Goal X, they must institute Program Y, requiring certain costs and resulting in certain consequences," Gans contends.[2]

Perhaps the greatest controversies in the field of planning have taken place over the issue of authority. Who should make planning decisions, and at what level of government should authority be invested?

Under the presidency of Lyndon B. Johnson during the 1960s, Great Society programs were begun to respond to urban plight and poverty. Federal governmental involvement in local community programs increased, as evidenced most dramatically by the Model Cities Program under the U.S. Department of Housing and Urban Development. Model Cities was intended to be a new federalism based on a partnership between federal, state, and local levels of authority. However, often there were conflicts between these levels of government, and the results were mixed. Speaking of the implications of urban renewal programs during this period, one sociologist has concluded: "At the cost of more than three billion dollars, the Urban Renewal Agency has succeeded in materially reducing the supply of low-cost housing in American cities."[3]

Unable to evaluate the effectiveness of the Great Society programs upon the quality of community life, policy makers turned to new approaches under the administration of Richard Nixon. Programs such as Model Cities were phased out and replaced by what was called revenue sharing—an attempt to return federal dollars to local communities. The new philosophy was based on the assumption that local communities know best their own problems and can spend funds wisely. However, the financial difficulties of most communities were underestimated; frequently local officials found it necessary to apply federal grants to maintaining existing services rather than using these funds to explore new services. As a part of the revenue-sharing program, a new dimension of planning—regionalism—developed, almost at times without local support or consideration. Cities and counties were obliged to join with other governments in order to receive funds. Supporters of regionalism argued that local services were simply too costly, and that if communities shared in the costs and operation of certain activities—such as the delivery of transportation services—programs could serve greater numbers of persons more efficiently. Opponents of regionalism could argue, on the other hand, that increasing the area of services might not increase their quality and might in fact remove control of expenditures from local control and evaluation.

Although regional approaches to planning now seem to predominate, there is another movement in community development that stresses decentralization, with planning at the local level. Community developer Milton Kotler, for example, argues that American neighborhoods have been exploited for the benefit of regionalism. He contends that "the fundamental character of the modern revolution has been local insurrection against the central power of the state,"[4] and suggests that neighborhoods control planning and funding of programs.

One Planning Model

The *Systematic Planning Model* below represents only one orderly planning process. On paper it appears to be systematic, but in reality the planning process does not always follow such a reasonable sequence of events.

Systematic Planning Model:

1. Assess needs.
2. Develop community support systems.
3. Set long- and short-range goals.
4. Select measurable objectives.
5. Determine priorities.
6. Design strategies.
7. Identify resources.
8. Operate programs.
9. Evaluate results.

Each of the above planning steps requires specific actions. How to *assess community needs* will be dealt with in the next section of this chapter. In *developing community support systems,* the planner looks for those networks of energy (other agencies, churches, schools) which will provide input into the planning process. It is essential, however, for representatives of the group primarily affected by the plan to be involved early in the process. *Goals* are simply statements that indicate ultimate purposes or directions; they can be long-range or short-range. *Objectives,* on the other hand, delineate specific actions needed to reach goals; they are measurable and always written in terms of clear outputs. For example, your goal might be to improve housing in your community. Your major objective might then be to reduce the percentage of substandard housing by 20 percent in four years.

It is always necessary to *select priorities* among the objectives set, recognizing the impossibility of realizing all goals within a short period of time but instead concentrating efforts on the attainment of major goals. Once objectives are set in priority, *strategies* are designed for carrying out programs. How you go about developing programs depends upon many factors, but *available resources* are crucial. It is difficult to develop programs for which there is neither community support nor resources.

Once programs are in operation for a period of time, it is necessary to *evaluate the results.* There are three basic types of evaluation: process, performance, and product. Process evaluation assesses programs developed over time: Who were the key actors and what events were crucial? Performance evaluation measures progress toward meeting objectives, for example: How many homes were brought up to code standards? Product evaluation asks the more difficult question: So what? What were the actual results of your efforts, and what difference do they make in your community?

Assessing the Needs of Older Adults

While few appreciate three-inch-thick research plans that gather dust and have little impact on the lives of people, it is necessary to understand the needs of older persons and to provide a way for each community to decide in what order the needs should be addressed. Many times there are common needs and priorities that cut across geographical divisions: income, transportation, health, nutrition; or as a retired teacher said during one discussion of needs: "You're a consumer before your're born, after you die, and every breath you take is at an inflated rate. If you solve the problem of inflation, you've solved all the rest."

How does one go about "assessing needs"? There are four possibilities suggested below:

1. Review existing information. In all probability the best source of information about the characteristics of older adults will be data from the U.S. Census Bureau; this will provide background on income, condition of housing, and related information. Local agencies in the community also retain information; for example, welfare departments should be able to describe Food Stamp use among older persons. *Before* initiating any new research, it is always wisest to review what is currently known.

2. Conduct research studies. The most direct way to assess needs and priorities is to ask questions directly of the persons to be served. It is reasonable to expect about 10 percent of those surveyed to respond.

3. Interview older persons. Because many older persons are isolated, even within large cities, it is often necessary to find ways of reaching out. In some communities, door-to-door interviews are conducted; this not only provides information but also serves as contact with isolated persons. Some agencies will use *longitudinal panels* to assess needs and evaluate programs. A longitudinal panel is a group selected and followed over time to see what impact programs have had. In one city, for example, some 150 older persons in a neighborhood were interviewed each six months over a three-year period. Another city arranged for interviews to be videotaped, and with the consent of the persons interviewed these tapes were compiled and used for training purposes.

4. Hold community meetings. It is important to provide informal forums where older persons can meet together to discuss needs and priorities. Before holding such meetings, it is best to recruit and train various persons as group moderators. In each session, records of the meeting should be taken. One interesting method to use in the meetings is to ask the participants to come up with a list of needs and priorities, and then actually vote to rank each one in order of importance.

No method of need assessment can succeed unless those whose needs are being reviewed are closely involved in the process. The role of the planner is not deciding what is best for persons, but assisting individuals in deriving their own assessments. In most cases, plans developed without broad community input and support end in failure.

Notes

1. Gans, Herbert J.: *People & Plans.* New York: Basic Books, 1968, p. ix.

2. Ibid., p. 81.

3. Banfield, Edward C.: *The Unheavenly City.* Boston: Little, Brown, 1970, p. 16.

4. Kotler, Milton: *Neighborhood Government.* Indianapolis: Bobbs-Merrill, 1969, p. 99.

8

Community Development and the Network on Aging

Concept, Context, and Process

The very mention of the concept of community development arouses disagreement. Arguments usually center on the meaning of *development.* Some stress the need for thoughtful, planned development within any social system—with a special emphasis on promoting developments that equalize opportunities within the community. Others, often associated with the environmental movement, seek to minimize development, particularly activities that appear to threaten the balance of nature. More than one zoning meeting has degenerated into a battle of words over whether or not development is required. Typically, debate centers on the question of new housing in previously undeveloped lands. Proponents of the housing argue that the city faces a severe shortage of adequate dwellings, while opponents counter that the land cannot stand such imbalances.

In the midst of arguments over whether or not development should be encouraged, many lose sight of a basic consideration: What is the nature of community? Wrestling with this question lays the groundwork for community development.

The issue of community development is especially important to those in the field of aging and older persons themselves, for aging takes place within a community context. The emphasis in planning and program development should be on how older persons can be encouraged and supported in their desire to remain active, productive community members. However, important as it is to have institutions for older persons no longer capable of caring for themselves, the primary consideration is to enable persons to remain independent rather than become institutionalized.

The key question to be considered, therefore, is: What is the meaning of a community? The responses to this question will determine in most cases issues surrounding development, particularly those that relate to the role played by older persons within the total community.

At its most elemental level, a community is a network of people who share certain common values and tend to live in close proximity to each other. Based on this definition, a community may be a neighborhood, town, city, county, region, or combination of any of these.

It is important to understand that a community is not a static reality but a dynamic process—a system for social action. For most, the community context is local, which means that the perimeters of interaction are limited to a particular geographical area. If one were to ask a person to identify his community, he would most likely name his town or city—not his nation. No matter how important it may be for some to promote the "community of humanity"—the recognition that the world is becoming a global village—the fact is that most of us tend to identify our communities within a very limited context.

The human situation is the prime consideration in any overview of community life. Each person occupies his or her own space; each has a unique history. But persons interact with each other and thereby form communities. Communities also involve organizations or networks of people. We often call these networks *institutions.* Seven of these central "institutions" are language, government, family, religion, knowledge and technology, recreation and the arts, and economics. To analyze community life, therefore, it is necessary to identify these sources of authority and to understand how they relate to each other.

The analysis of communities is a growing field of research, and space does not permit a detailed description of the complexities involved. Nonetheless, the community context is the arena in which responses to the issues of aging must be addressed, for the problems of growing old are not only individual but also collective, requiring community involvement, resources, and development.

Asking the Right Questions

The needs of older persons cannot be seen apart from the communities in which they live. For this reason, programs must develop out of an awareness of the history, culture, resources, and limitations of the community. A list of the general types of questions to be asked about the characteristics of the local community is developed below:

1. How many persons are there over the age of 65 and what percentage of the population does this figure represent?
2. Where are the largest concentrations of persons 65 and over?
3. What percentage of those over 65 is considered below the poverty level? What are their characteristics?
4. What percentage of those 65 and over is a head of household? How many reside in institutions (nursing homes, public housing)?
5. How many older persons are dependent solely on Social Security for their income?
6. How many minority older persons are there in the community? For how many is English a second language?
7. How many older persons in the community are using Food Stamps? How many more are eligible?
8. How many of those 65 and over are employed full-time? Part-time? Are any special employment considerations extended to older persons by any private or public agency?
9. Are there any businesses that do not have mandatory retirement policies? If so, what are their plans?
10. Are there any organized attempts to provide volunteer opportunities for older persons?
11. How many services are available in the community to enable older persons to remain independent rather than institutionalized?
12. Does your community have special housing for older persons? If so, are there long waiting lists for entrance?
13. Is there accessible, low-cost transportation specifically designed for older persons?
14. Is there any counseling service especially set up for older adults?
15. What special projects have been financed with the community's revenue-sharing funds?
16. How accessible are health care services to the concentrations of older persons?
17. What institutional facilities (nursing homes, adult day care centers, county homes) are available?
18. What organizations exist solely for the purpose of serving older persons? How effective have they been?
19. Do any educational institutions provide special programs for older adults?

20. How do older persons in the community gain access to political power?
21. What percentage of homes owned by older persons is considered "substandard"?
22. How many and what kinds of nutrition programs are there?

These are the types of questions that must be addressed in any meaningful planning process, but each community has its own particular issues. It is of particular importance, therefore, that these questions be raised in groups which are informal and open and in which older persons have a voice. There is a normal tendency among community leaders to want to believe that older persons are "taken care of," and for this reason formulation of the questions may itself cause disagreement and conflict. But without conflict there is no competition for new ways of doing things.

Establishing Priorities

Those in planning professions often confuse the product of their efforts with the process. Possible products are improvements in housing, education, health, transit. All of these may be necessary, but the process of planning is to repair, uplift, and promote *human* development. New housing inhabited by unfulfilled human beings is hardly an achievement, just as educating persons to feel useless is self-defeating. The first principle of planning—the one often forgotten—is to promote human growth in all its diversity.

It is necessary to establish priorities during the planning process, because funds are always limited and cannot meet every need, institutions cannot accomplish every objective at the same time, and time is best spent working on major areas of need rather than being scattered across a thousand concerns. Each community needs to center attention on its own priorities; however, there are some national priorities for older persons, and these are discussed below.

1. Adequate income. The lack of income necessary to sustain basic life needs can have devastating physical and psychological effects. A significant percentage of older persons live in poverty, while millions of other on fixed incomes find living a struggle to survive.

2. Accessible, low-cost health care. Older persons are said to account for about 25 percent of the nation's health expenditures, yet for many older adults health remains a continual worry—particularly the fear of catastrophic illness which requires lengthy hospitalization at great cost. Preventative medical health, which would include regular examinations and health monitoring, would go a long way toward lessening the terrible impact of prolonged illness.

3. *Opportunities for creativity and leisure activities.* Persons in retirement years require opportunities to continue to use skills gained over a lifetime and to develop talents.

4. *Employment adapted to individual requirements.* Individuals should be permitted the right to continue employment as long as they remain effective; mandatory retirement is a form of ageism. But employment should be diversified: full-time, part-time, or consultative.

5. *Accessible transportation tailored to the requirements of older persons.* Community services and opportunities are useless if individuals are not mobile. Often, older persons cannot afford the rising costs of owning an automobile, and thus are dependent upon public transit or other systems, such as friends and neighbors or taxicabs. In many cases transportation must be especially suited to the age group, such as provision of door-to-door service or vehicles equipped with low stairs and handrails.

6. *Access to information, resources, and community decision-making.* Because of the complexity of services available at the community level, older persons may fail to use existing resources. Promoting a reliable, current flow of information is essential to the success of various community services.

7. *Adequate provision of nutritional services on a daily basis.* Adequate nutritional intake each day is a prerequisite to physical and mental well-being; yet because of economic factors, poorer older adults often do not have proper food. Meals delivered to the homes of older persons who are isolated and meals served at a central location are both required.

8. *Moderately priced housing or alternatives to permit remaining in one's own home.* The vast majority of older persons live in their own homes; yet the rising costs of homeownership make it extremely difficult for many others to remain in their own dwellings. Efforts can be made to provide ways for individuals to remain in their own homes (property tax discounts, home repair services) or, at the very least, to provide alternatives to institutions (retirement housing, communes, homebound services).

9. *Freedom from personal threats to well-being.* Older persons are more often victimized by crime than is any other age group. Crimes against older persons involve not only bodily assaults, but the more subtle crime of consumer fraud.

10. Systematic, organized support for the goals of older adults. Because older persons have traditionally been perceived as powerless, a network of organizations is required which derive their strength from older persons themselves and which work on their behalf in a coordinated manner.

Community Development and the Aging Network

Although various federal, state, and local programs for older adults have existed for some time, it was not until the passage of the Older Americans Act in 1965 that an attempt was made to initiate a network on aging, which attempted to link together previously uncoordinated activities and authorized the establishment of state offices on aging. These state offices provided funds to various community agencies to provide services to older adults.

The amendments to the Act in 1973 changed the focus of the network from a state and local effort to include regional Area Agencies on Aging. The developing network on aging now included the federal, state, regional, and local agencies.

The federal component of the network is the Administration on Aging, located within the Department of Health, Education and Welfare. Each state has initiated its own office on aging; some states, such as Ohio, have set up commissions on aging while others, such as Massachusetts, have developed departments on aging within state government. Each state is required by law to have an advisory council composed of a majority of consumers of service, whose task it is to review plans and offer suggestions on programs.

Although some states, such as New Hampshire, maintain only a state office on aging, most have created regional structures to plan and develop programs. Two of the more important regional units within the network are Area Agencies on Aging and Title VII nutrition agencies. Area Agencies on Aging are principally responsible for the planning and administration of grants under Title III of the Older Americans Act, which provides funds for a broad range of social services. Title VII agencies are chiefly held accountable for the development of nutritional services to older persons. Where possible, states attempt to designate one regional agency to administer both Title III and Title VII funds, although this is not always the case.

According to federal regulations, area agencies have six basic functions:

1. To provide leadership and advocacy on behalf of older persons.
2. To determine the need for services within the region, with particular stress placed on the needs of minority and low-income older adults.
3. To develop an inventory of services already available to older persons in the region.
4. To establish a plan of action for meeting the unmet needs of the older persons in the region.
5. To coordinate existing services within the area.
6. To develop new services in the region, principally by contracting with existing agencies to perform services.

Area agencies are principally responsible for the administration of Title III grants under the Older Americans Act; these funds are to be used to assist older persons in maintaining independence. Types of services that may be funded under Title III include health, continuing education, information and referral, homemaker, counseling, transportation, housing, legal assistance, and other social services designed to promote independence. Like the state agencies, each area agency is required to select an advisory council of persons to review needs and to help identify potential projects, a majority of whom must be consumers of services provided by the area agency.

Title VII nutrition agencies are principally responsible for providing meals to older adults. Each Title VII agency establishes nutrition sites within the region where groups of older persons may gather; a small percentage of the effort may also be directed toward the provision of meals-on-wheels projects. Each Title VII agency is also required to establish an advisory council.

While state and regional Area Agencies on Aging and Title VII agencies are the most visible components of the aging network, there are other equally viable parts of the system at the community level. Such organizations as the American Association of Retired Persons (AARP) have long been active in the aging network at the federal, state, and local levels. More important, towns and cities have recently established locally based councils on aging, many of which are closely tied to government units. These councils, many of which are composed mainly of older citizens in the community, seek to identify local needs and urge the support of local officials in developing resources to provide services. Finally, coalitions of older persons are forming to work as advocates for the needs of the aged. Such an organization is the Gray Panthers, which seeks the involvement of younger persons too in their lobbying efforts, in the belief that community programs and legislation have implications for all age groups.

It is important to realize that the issues of aging are not limited to organizations directly involved with the concerns of the older person, such as Area Agencies on Aging, but involve the whole community network—public and private agencies, voluntary associations, and all phases of government operation. The financial and staff resources of most organizations in the field of aging are simply too limited to require that they become the sole catalysts for development of programs for the aging. Health and welfare agencies, for example, may redirect their own resources to meet the needs of older citizens; health departments may decide to provide free health assessment and information, specifically tailored to older adults, while welfare departments may engage in more vigorous outreach to the isolated aged population to make certain they receive the benefits to which they are entitled. Voluntary associations, such as churches or civic clubs, may also commit time and support to developing projects in the field of aging; some churches, for example, find it economically feasible and desirable to utilize their facilities as sites for senior centers or nutrition sites. Governmental bodies are becoming aware of their responsibilities to older citizens; in terms of financial support, a network of public funding exists that may be tapped for community services. For example, in one community a transportation service was developed for older citizens using a combination of funding sources: vehicles were purchased under funds from the federal revenue-sharing program, drivers were paid out of monies from the federal Comprehensive Employment and Training Act, and general operating costs were paid out of county and municipal funds.

Integration into Community Life

The principal focus of Title III of the Older Americans Act is to assist older persons in remaining independent—which means essentially to remain productive members of their communities. Rather than segregating persons because of age into "senior citizen" housing or centers, a major objective of many newer programs has been to find ways to promote integration of older adults into the patterns of community life with which they are familiar. How this integrating process is taking place varies from city to city, and projects engendered by funds from the Older Americans Act have been imaginative, if not always successful. While it is impossible to cover all of the projects attempted, it is interesting to note the diversity of a few.

Some states, such as Massachusetts and Connecticut, sought to develop what is called "single entry" systems for social services, in which homecare corporations or the like were designed to provide an agency that would serve as a central clearinghouse for the provision of services. In the past, persons seeking services might have to sort through a multiplicity of agencies—and might end up, if they were fortunate enough to find what they required, receiving fragmented help from many sources. Under the single-entry system, the homecare agency serves as a central point of contact for the individual seeking assistance and then serves as a broker for making certain that the help requested is given. Proponents of this type of service-delivery system argue that it provides the support older adults need to remain in their own communities rather than entering nursing homes.

Other areas have pioneered in the development of special transportation systems for older persons. The approach most often developed has been called "dial-a-ride" or "community response transit," which is based on the special needs of older persons. Rather than being fixed route systems in which bus service is maintained over the same route on a daily basis, dial-a-ride transit often involves door-to-door service. Generally, an agency provides a central phone number within the community which can be called for service; in most cases, transportation can be provided within a short time on the same day, often through the use of vehicles that are especially equipped with handrails or low steps for easy access. The service is used for transportation to doctors or hospital clinics, grocery stores, or other points within the community. The implementation of many of these systems has been remarkably innovative. Churches, for example, have joined together to purchase buses and may even provide volunteer drivers from their own congregations. Local governments often provide funds to purchase the vehicles required, with funds for the costs of drivers and fuel coming from Area Agencies on Aging. In Wellington, Ohio, the senior citizens together with the village council purchased a special bus and then utilized their own police-dispatching service as the call-in point for rides. In other areas, with the passage of special state legislation, school buses have been used in off-hours for older adults, while other towns have found it possible to provide subsidies to local taxi companies to provide rides at a reduced rate for persons over the age of 60.

Other programs developed to help older persons maintain their independence have been in geriatric health care, although this area is only beginning to be addressed. A typical approach is that of Lorain County, Ohio, where a specially trained nurse with staff works to provide free health checkups and assessment of health status in community sites throughout the area—churches, public housing sites, community centers, and other accessible locations. Other agencies have utilized different approaches, such as providing a visiting nurse who actually visits the client's home.

Income for the aged continues to be a pressing problem. Social planners may argue that adequate financial resources are the key to personal satisfaction, that if an older adult has a stable economic base, services required may be purchased on the open market. Positive approaches to meeting this need most frequently rest on national policies, such as increased Social Security income or the lifting of restrictions on employment past a certain age. Two types of model projects have attempted to address the issue of income, although these do not answer the question of inadequate financial resources among a significant number of persons 60 years of age and older. One approach is that of continued employment into the later years of life. Some agencies have utilized funds from either Title IX of the Older Americans Act or the Comprehensive Employment and Training Act to provide part-time jobs for persons 60 years of age or older. In most cases, jobs must be part-time because there continues to be a restriction on the amount of job-related income a person on Social Security may earn without losing benefits. Other agencies have sought to promote projects that have indirect impact on the economic security of older adults. For example, social service agencies may mount aggressive outreach efforts to alert older adults of services to which they are entitled. For example, within the past few years some agencies have tried to increase older adult participation in the Food Stamp or supplemental Social Security programs. Another popular approach has been to establish discount programs whereby an older person may be given a price reduction on certain goods and services. The State of Ohio, for example, has developed a single discount program for all persons 65 years of age and older. While a discount project cannot substitute for real income, some smaller communities have initiated rather comprehensive programs.

Although projects related to the need for housing among older adults have been planned for many years, new approaches to this issue are also developing. The traditional approach to this problem is to construct special housing projects for older persons, usually involving full or partial funding from the Department of Housing and Urban Development. While there is an obvious need for such housing and rental costs are low, it must be pointed out that the creation of separate facilities for older persons increases age segregation in the community rather than providing for a mix of ages in the general population. On a smaller scale, some communities have opted for housing projects that promote integration and stability.

Beginning from the premise that most older homeowners would rather remain in their own houses than enter a housing project or other institutional setting, agencies have developed projects to support the maintenance of the private dwelling. Some agencies provide home repair services—such as painting or minor plumbing—to older homeowners. Many times, retired carpenters or skilled laborers are employed to do the work. In cold climates agencies have provided funds to eligible older homeowners to insulate their houses, thus cutting down on heating costs. A more infrequent attempt, by voluntary associations such as churches or neighborhood groups, has been to operate private homes for more than one older resident. An older house may be restored and made available to persons over a certain age, who share in the work of the home as if they were a family.

Social planners generally believe that adequate nutrition is essential to personal well-being and stability. Title VII nutrition programs provide the major activities in this area, but other approaches have been carried out. For example, in some states school cafeterias are used during off-hours as food sites for older persons, while churches in other areas provide meals at their facility or send meals to the homes of older adults unable to come to a central site.

Within the past few years, educational institutions have also begun to redirect their efforts in the areas of continuing education and leisure activities for older citizens. Many states provide tuition-free learning to older residents, while others design courses of special interest to retired persons who want to pursue a course of instruction for their own benefit or to prepare for a new career in the retirement years.

While many communities are beginning to address themselves to ways to integrate older adults into the mainstream of life, the efforts now being made are still in the infancy stage. Much can be done on a small scale, utilizing volunteer support and limited funds from private agencies and local governments. But the projects being developed cannot expand without continued and concentrated support from all levels of the network: federal, state, and local. Under the Older Americans Act, for example, projects funded under Title III are for a limited period of time; since funds generally decrease each year, local support must be found to continue. With local governments and private agencies experiencing financial difficulties themselves, it is difficult to maintain services much less expand them. For this reason, persons working in the field of aging often urge that a national policy on aging be adopted, to be funded at a level consistent with the needs of older persons.

9

Outreach and Communications with Older Persons

The Outreach Role Defined

The best programs for older persons are ineffective unless individuals are aware of services provided and avail themselves of assistance. Very often, at the community level, older persons express frustration at not being made aware of existing services. It can reasonably be expected that in the coming years as the percentage of the population over the age of 60 increases, there may be a corresponding growth in special services directed toward older persons. It is vital, therefore, that an effective communications and outreach system be in place to close the gap between services available and human needs.

In many respects, the development of effective outreach and communications efforts in the field of aging is in its infancy, in spite of the existence of literally thousands of program workers whose responsibilities include outreach. Part of the difficulty is that the concept of outreach is confusing. One organization may define outreach in terms of *information dissemination,* which means alerting potential service users to what is available. Other groups take a more aggressive approach to outreach as a *service provision,* and consider outreach ineffective unless a specific service is actually provided to meet a special need. Many agencies have specific staff, often called outreach workers, whose task is to close the gap between available services and the needs of clients. Other agencies consider outreach a more general function, which each staff member must undertake.

Although no widely accepted definition of outreach exists, one organization attempted to define the outreach role according to four levels of responsibility for the worker:[1]

Level I

• Do outreach visits or calls to homes, families, and neighborhoods to detect people, help them to understand the problem, and motivate them to seek help.

• Assess and decide how to best handle problem.

• Do outreach to follow up clients and assure that they are progressing with their rehabilitation in the community.

• Make self available—not just be available.

• Work with families at home or in office to help implement services and interpret laws, policies, and regulations.

Level II

• Reach out to small groups for detection of problems and understanding.

• Reach out to organize and follow up groups.

• Reach out to work with persons who are unable to come to services.

Level III

• Reach out to community groups and agencies to help them appreciate and manage psychosocial problems.

Level IV

• Reach out to major agencies, industries, etc., to help them identify, analyze, and solve psychosocial problems.

From this rather universal definition of the responsibilities of the outreach worker, various generalizations can be drawn about the functions of outreach:

1. Outreach is an attempt to alert individuals and groups to the availability of services to meet their needs.
2. Outreach involves the dissemination of information, assessment of human needs, and referral or provision of services to meet identified needs.
3. Outreach involves the attempt to mobilize community resources to identify problems for which there is no immediate solution and to work toward initiating new services.

Closing the Gap

The major objective of any outreach program is to close the gap between services available and the needs of persons. In the field of aging, major outreach efforts were initiated with the passage of the

Older Americans Act in 1965, although more general outreach efforts had been required under both the Model Cities and Community Action programs during the late 1960s. One case study of the outreach efforts in the Model Cities Program, completed over a two-year period, in a city in which every household in the service area was personally visited by an outreach worker, uncovered some interesting findings.[2] First, although needs were catalogued, the overwhelming majority of those contacted had little awareness of existing services. Second, even when individuals were aware of existing services, there was a great reluctance to use them; in many cases, individuals felt wary of any agency service, and particularly among older residents there was a strong sense of independence and unwillingness to rely on others. Third, and perhaps of most importance, it was found that individual needs were often being met in an informal, neighborly way. Persons interviewed felt more comfortable seeking help from family or friends. This becomes an important reality in outreach efforts, for it should mean to those in the field that wherever possible this informal structure of assistance should be supported and developed, and that agency intervention should take place only where no other help is available.

The Older Americans Act, which funds a wide range of state and local programs for older persons, places a priority on the development of *information and referral* services in each community. Information and referral is one major outreach function, as has been previously noted. Typically, an information and referral system works in the following way: a resource directory or guide to existing community services is compiled and used as a basic reference. Trained workers become familiar with the guide and with various interviewing techniques. In most cases the initial contact with persons seeking assistance is over the telephone. After listening to the caller's request carefully, the worker consults the directory and serves as a broker between the services available and the caller's needs. Records of all incoming calls are kept, and usually there is a follow-up process to make certain the service was received. Not all information and referral services are performed over the telephone; some home visits may be performed. However, typically, information and referral is a telephone service. The traditional criticism of this type of service is that it cannot always provide the services requested, and that in some major areas—particularly financial—there simply are not enough resources available to meet demands. However, it should be noted that this criticism must then be applied across the board, since it is not the purpose of information and referral to provide direct services, but only to serve as a clearinghouse between agencies and clients.

The relationship between information and referral and outreach should be obvious since both deal with the broad area of communications. In one sense, information and referral skills are required by the outreach worker, who must have a sense of community resources and be able to refer persons in the field. Both seek information about the individual as well, in order to assess carefully what services are actually required. Outreach workers, however, are required literally to reach out to individuals wherever they live, organize groups around some common issues, and provide assistance to institutions in identifying problems to be resolved.

While social visionaries hope for the time when there will be no gap between human needs and societal response, the outreach effort must be tempered with the knowledge that there simply are not enough resources now available to meet all current needs. For this reason, outreach efforts should be directed at both the individual and group levels.

Conducting a Needs Assessment

Prior to the initiation of programs, the argument goes, an outreach effort must be made to assess the needs of the potential group to be served; at the often frantic level of planning programs, however, needs assessment often turns out to be justification for programs already planned, although this need not be the case. Again, the difficulty with carrying out a needs assessment comes back to language: What is a "need"?

One retired member of a citizens' advisory board once remarked that although he had been teaching for over 50 years, he was never sure if his students grasped the difference between "needs" and "wants." To oversimplify his case, he said that a need was a service required to live, a want was a fantasy no one could fulfill. Two generalizations could be made concerning human needs: first, there are different perceptions of what constitutes a need; and second, needs change over time. In a 1976 needs assessment in one Ohio county, older residents identified their major needs as adequate income, accessible transportation, and preventive health care. While there was some variation in the order of priority of these three needs according to age, race, and income, there was some general consensus that these were essential needs of older persons. At the same time, however, among *providers* of service there was a perceived need for emotional-support services for older persons. There is a tendency to confuse *felt needs* (what the service provider feels is needed) and *expressed needs* (what the service user says is needed). Felt needs are often latent in the community; expressed needs, on the other hand, are more concrete and overt.

There are two basic needs assessment philosophies. The first is *objective;* it seeks to measure needs statistically or empirically (how many persons are low-income, how many persons require health assistance, etc.). The second approach is *subjective;* it asks individuals or groups which needs are most important. The most frequently used approach is still the social survey, which usually involves a questionnaire or interviews with a sample group from a larger community. Researchers generally find that a combination of both approaches is required for even a rudimentary grasp of needs. In some areas assessment interviews are conducted by specially trained older persons. Social planners also use *case studies* to assess needs and evaluate the results of various programs. In this approach, a sample grouping of persons is interviewed and then interviewed again after a certain passage of time to see how needs have changed or whether services have had any impact on quality of life.

Another interesting approach to assessing the needs of older persons is called the *index of incapacity.* The approach is based on the assumption that the self-reports of older persons as to what they can and cannot do are reliable means of assessing the need for services. Older persons involved in this type of assessment are asked simple questions: Can you go up and down the stairs? Can you feed and clothe yourself? The results of this approach are then used to determine what services might be required to keep the older adult independent. By way of a general conclusion, it might be said that most needs assessments show that those older persons living alone and without family supports usually tend to require more services.

Community Outreach Principles

For many years the predominant mode of outreach was at the individual level: detecting persons with problems, assessing these problems, and then seeking solutions. Critics have argued that this approach sought to foster dependency on inadequate social systems, noting that it made little sense to promote individual adjustment if the entire social order was unjust. In his book *Crisis in Black and*

White, Charles E. Silberman attacked this emphasis on individuality:

> Social workers, in particular, have made Freud their God when they should have been worshipping at the shrine of the sociologist Emile Durkheim. For the problems of the slum stem less from individual neuroses (though certainly there are plenty of those) than from an objective lack of opportunity, from a social system that denies that individual dignity and status.[3]

The tasks of social work also apply to outreach. The *enabler* or *broker* role assumes that the job of the social worker or outreach worker is to provide a link between available services and human needs. The broker, after all, begins with the belief that individuals can define their own needs—and that these needs can be addressed through existing channels. A second role is that of *advocate,* the assumption being that for whatever reason, existing resources cannot or will not meet needs. In the advocacy role the outreach worker moves beyond individual assistance, seeking to involve groups of people around felt or expressed needs in order to promote change.

Whatever role model is adopted, and probably both will need to be used by the outreach worker, some common traits were found by two researchers among outreach workers in youth programs. "A major reason for success," they say, "was that the outreach worker expected the youths to do well, involved them in the planning and implementation of the program, and held himself responsible if the program failed."[4]

There are some general concepts of community outreach programs that take into account both the enabler and advocate roles; these principles are related to outreach efforts directed toward older adults.

1. *An effective outreach program begins from a knowledge base that takes into account the special needs and priorities of the group to be served.* From this starting point, outreach workers should be trained in understanding the aging process and should have a grasp of the basic statistics of the group to be served (from a needs assessment). Some agency directors feel that the best outreach workers are those who have experienced many of the same problems as those of the group to be served, and for this reason they will often select older persons to be outreach workers.
2. *An effective program of outreach begins with an awareness of existing community resources.* Obviously, if outreach

workers are to serve as information and referral agents, they must understand what community resources are available to assist clients. This must include knowledge of both *formal* and *informal* resources within the community. Formal resources include institutional services, such as health and welfare or Social Security. Informal resources include family and friends, churches, or other helpers outside the agency structure.

3. *An effective outreach program seeks to involve clients in the planning and development of services.* The typical complaint against caseworkers is that they tend to be paternalistic—that is, they tend to define needs in terms of their own rather than the clients' requirements. Effective outreach begins with the assumption that the individual to be served has rights and is in the best position to define needs. The outreach worker, therefore, plans *with* people rather than *for* them.
4. *An effective outreach program provides for evaluation.* Evaluation is typically conceived of as taking place at the end of a program; but, in fact, evaluation begins at the initiation of a service. An effective outreach program begins with the selection of certain clear, measurable objectives (such as, within six months 2000 persons 60 years of age and older will receive transportation services which previously they did not receive). By setting such clear outreach objectives in the beginning, it becomes possible to evaluate the effectiveness of the outreach effort.

Informal Outreach: An Untapped Potential

The tendency is to think of outreach only in terms of formal functions of an agency with paid staff serving as outreach workers. But in the normal routines of living, individuals are engaged in outreach, even if these persons are not traditionally thought of as outreach workers. Effective planners seek to utilize these informal outreach processes in innovative ways. Some of these informal processes are identified below.

1. In England, outreach functions are fulfilled by milkmen in some areas. If the milkman finds that an older person is not taking in the milk delivered, he alerts a social service agency, and an outreach worker is dispatched to the house.

2. In a few areas of the United States, particularly in rural areas, mailmen function as outreach workers. Since they are familiar with persons on their routes, they are able to keep track of isolated older persons and refer any problems to appropriate agencies.
3. In one program on aging, an agreement was worked out with the regional phone company and an information and referral service. Since it was known that over 80 percent of the older persons in that area had telephones, the phone company agreed to send information about services in their monthly billing statements—together with a sticker to be placed on the telephone which included the names and phone numbers of agencies with special services to older individuals.
4. In Lorain County, Ohio, a discount program registered some 23,000 older persons. A group of retired persons themselves then began to phone each individual on the list, informing them of new services and checking to make certain they were receiving financial benefits to which they were entitled. In a three-month period, over 4000 individuals were contacted, about one-third of whom were found to be eligible for new benefits.

The use of informal outreach workers is limited only by the imagination of those planning programs. Other potential outreach agents might include:

1. Druggists. Drug stores often deliver prescription items to the homes of older persons. Information about other health benefits could be delivered at the same time.
2. Clergy. Often, clergy are points of contact with many older members of their congregations and could be used to carry information and materials to isolated individuals.
3. Hospitals. Hospitals keep records of older persons who have been discharged and who are often in need of assistance during recovery.
4. Neighbors. Some offices on aging have developed neighborhood volunteer workers on a block-by-block basis; their role is simply to monitor the progress of their older neighbors and report any difficulties to social service agencies.
5. Police Departments. One smaller community utilized its police department dispatching center as a contact point for older persons in the community. The community operated

a dial-a-ride bus service for older persons, using the police dispatcher as a calling point to request rides. The dispatcher soon found himself as a central information point for disseminating information and receiving requests for help.

Outreach is only as effective as the quality of services offered. If the consumer of services is dissatisfied, no amount of outreach will increase utilization.

The key question of outreach, therefore, must involve the quality of services offered. If those planning and administering programs would find no difficulty in using their own services, there is some indication that the service offered is adequate. Unfortunately, in many cases those administering programs would not want to be in the position of receiving their own services. For example, in a survey of health professionals in 1976, over 40 percent indicated that they would not want to be consumers of their own service.

The whole question of outreach relates to the entire issue of aging in culture. Until those providing service gain a measure of enlightened self-interest in understanding that they are also consumers, outreach efforts will lead only to frustrated and dissatisfied users of service.

Notes

1. Schulman, Eveline D.: *Intervention in Human Services.* St. Louis: C. V. Mosby, 1974, p. 6.

2. Morgan, John C.: "A Hundred Percent Demographic Survey of a Model Cities Neighborhood." 1969.

3. Silberman, Charles E.: *Crisis in Black and White.* New York: Vintage Books, 1964, p. 312.

4. Bannon, Joseph J.: *Outreach: Extending Community Services in Urban Areas.* Springfield, Ill.: Charles C. Thomas, 1973, p. 53.

Appendix

Developing Resources for the Study and Practice of Gerontology

Becoming Old has been written from the point of view of one learner exploring with other learners. This focus arises from the awareness of the need for learning experiences that are both varied and related to the world in which persons live and work. Unfortunately, in gerontology as in other areas of study, learning has been seen as what takes place in the classroom three hours each week over the period of a few months. Given this perception, educational experiences tend to take on the characteristics of information processing, storage, and possible recall—learning of the "piggy bank" variety, which assumes that students have small slits in the backs of their heads into which information is poured on a somewhat regular basis. For those accustomed to this mode of instruction, the materials in this book may cause some frustration, simply because the burden of learning is placed on the learner.

This book is but one "instructor" in the study of gerontology. Persons will need to explore the issues of aging from many sources: the classroom experience or training session, past experience in the field of aging, present work experience if involved as a staff member or volunteer in the field of aging, and experiences with older persons themselves. It is one of the major assumptions of the author that learning about aging cannot take place in isolation from encounters with the aging process itself, either in a personal way or at the community level.

If learning is a personal responsibility, the key to success is the preliminary identification of resources available. This appendix is a beginning point in developing a resource directory for the study of gerontology. As individuals continue their own studies, they will find it easier to identify and collect additional materials.

Periodicals

Aging. U.S. Department of Health, Education and Welfare, Administration on Aging, Washington, D.C. 20402.

Aging and Work. National Council on the Aging, 1828 L Street, N.W., Washington, D.C. 20036.

American Association of Retired Persons News Bulletin. Dupont Circle Building, Washington, D.C. 20036.

Educational Gerontology. Hemisphere Publishing Corp., 1025 Vermont Avenue, N.W., Washington, D.C. 20005.

The Gerontologist. One Dupont Circle, Washington, D.C. 20036.

Journal of Geriatric Psychiatry. International Universities Press, Inc., 239 Park Avenue South, N.Y., N.Y. 10003.

Journal of Gerontological Nursing. Charles B. Slack Publications, Thorofare, New Jersey 08086.

Journal of Gerontology. One Dupont Circle, Washington, D.C. 20036.

Journal of Long Term Care Administration. American College of Nursing Home Administrators, 4650 East-West Highway, Washington, D.C. 20014.

Perspective on Aging. National Council on the Aging, 1828 L Street, N.W., Washington, D.C. 20036.

Social Casework. Family Service Association of America, 44 East 23rd Street, N.Y., N.Y. 10010.

Social Security Bulletin. Government Printing Office, Washington, D.C. 20402.

Social Welfare Reform. National Conference on Social Welfare, 22 West Gay Street, Columbus, Ohio 43215.

Urban Affairs Quarterly. 275 South Beverly Drive, Beverly Hills, California 90212.

Organizations Related to Older Persons

Federal

Administration on Aging, Department of Health, Education and Welfare, 330 C Street, S.W., Washington, D.C. Administers all titles of the Older Americans Act and serves as a national clearinghouse for information related to aging programs.

National Institute on Aging, Department of Health, Education and Welfare. Established under the National Institutes of Health to increase knowledge of the aging process.

Social Security Administration, Department of Health, Education and Welfare. Administers Medicare, Social Security, and retirement benefits.

National

American Association of Homes for the Aging, Room 374, National Press Building, Washington, D.C. Relates on a national basis to the broad interests of nonprofit homes for the aging.

American Association of Retired Persons, 1225 Connecticut Avenue, N.W., Washington, D.C. Publishes regular newspaper, offers special projects, and advises on legislation.

American Geriatrics Society, 10 Columbus Circle, New York, N.Y. Publishes journal of American Geriatrics Society.

American Nursing Home Association, 1025 Connecticut Avenue, N.W., Suite 607, Washington, D.C. Publishes newsletter and monthly magazine; deals with licensed nursing homes in North America.

Gerontological Society, One Dupont Circle, Washington, D.C. Publishes *The Gerontologist;* provides training in aging and promotes the application of research to public policy. Also publishes *The Journal of Gerontology.*

Gray Panthers, 6342 Green Street, Philadelphia, Pa. National organization for all age groups concerned with the problems of older persons; active in legislation and community organization.

National Caucus on the Black Aged, Inc., 1725 DeSales, Washington, D.C. Concerned primarily with the needs of minority aged; publishes periodicals and develops program resources.

National Center for Voluntary Action, 1785 Massachusetts Avenue, N.W., Washington, D.C. Clearinghouse for voluntary activities and projects, including those for older persons.

National Council of Senior Citizens, Inc., 1627 K Street, N.W., Washington, D.C. Provides information, workshops, part-time employment, and a monthly newspaper for members.

National Council on the Aging, Inc., 1828 L Street, N.W., Washington, D.C. National, voluntary organization providing leadership services for organizations and individuals concerned with aging; publishes a bimonthly newsletter.

National Retired Teachers Association, 1225 Connecticut Avenue, N.W., Washington, D.C. Provides services to retired and former educators; acts on legislative matters.

Other Community Resources in Aging

In addition to governmental programs in the field of aging there are other agencies and organizations that provide services to older adults at the community level. A few of the more active are included here; individuals interested in such organizations should contact a local chapter or unit.

Senior Centers. These are multipurpose centers at the local level which provide a wide variety of services to older adults. Typical of activities provided are crafts and volunteer opportunities, nutrition, continuing education, group trips, and other socializing events. Most communities now have senior centers, which are often supported with local tax revenues.

Churches. Many churches not only provide services to members of their own congregations but also to the wider community. Church facilities may be used for a senior center site or a nutrition center. In addition, within their budgets, churches are beginning to develop other activities for older adults, such as telephone reassurance or visitation programs.

Schools. All levels of the educational network can become resources for older-adult programs. Public grade and high schools may be utilized as nutrition or recreation sites, or offer adult education projects. Colleges may also offer free use of library facilities, free-tuition courses, consumer information, health-screening programs, and career training.

Voluntary associations. Voluntary associations are those that depend mainly on the support of volunteers who may pay dues or assist in the operation of programs. One of the more active volunteer organizations with local chapters is the American Association of Retired Persons (AARP), which now numbers 3000 local organizations and a combined membership of over 11 million persons. Members of the AARP are given the opportunity to participate in a broad range of activities, from group travel to community service projects. Within each community, as well, other voluntary associations such as retirement clubs and senior citizen councils promote activities.

Additional Readings in Aging

Each year the number of books in the field of gerontology continues to increase, so much so that it is difficult for a beginning student to know where to begin exploring resources. A good beginning point for additional reading is obviously a local public or educational library, but a few basic resources are listed here:

Aging and Behavior: A Comprehensive Integration of Research Findings. Second Edition. Botwinick, Jack. New York: Springer Publishing Company, 1978.

Clinical Aspects of Aging: A Comprehensive Text Prepared Under the Direction of the American Geriatrics Society. Baltimore: Williams and Wilkins, 1978.

Current Literature on Aging. A quarterly subject guide to selected new publications in aging, published by the National Council on the Aging, 1828 L Street, N.W., Washington, D.C. 20036.

Gerontology: An Annotated Bibliography. Rook, M. Leigh and Wingrove, C. Ray. Washington, D.C.: University Press of America, 1977.

Films and Audiotapes

An excellent resource for identifying films of special interest is *About Aging: A Catalog of Films.* Los Angeles: Andrus Gerontology Center, University of Southern California, University Park, California.

Case Studies

A case study is a written record of the key actors, issues, and decisions in the life of an individual or organization. Because these are records of actual events, they become excellent ways to assess skills in understanding, interpreting, and deciding upon problems presented. Social service agencies may have on file fictionalized case studies, based on actual experiences in the field. Two sample case studies are given here.

Case Study I: Mrs. K. is 68 years old and has been living alone for the past five years since her husband died. Although she receives social security benefits, her income has been drastically reduced by rising costs of keeping up her home, most especially heat and light. Because of a savings account in her name, she has been declared over the income limit for certain benefits, such as homemaker and health services in her own home. Her only daughter lives in another state, and rarely visits. Mrs. K. has Parkinson's Disease, and is unable to prepare her own meals with any degree of regularity. *Question:* If you were the caseworker called in for the first time to visit Mrs. K., how would you deal with her problems and what might you recommend?

Case Study II: An Area Agency on Aging, with an annual budget of $190,000 of Title III, Older Americans Act funds, has recently evaluated its programs. The evaluation report indicated a low rate of participation among lower-income elderly. The agency has undergone a series of internal conflicts, including the removal of its director and the resignations of four board members. Over half of the agency budget for the past three years has been used to develop transportation services for the some 60,000 individuals in the region 60 years of age and older. Recently, a new director was hired, and given six months to increase the levels of participation of low-income older persons within the agency programs. *Question:* If you were hired as the new director, what steps would you take to meet the six-month requirement?

Community Projects as Learning Experiences

In order to understand the issues of aging, particularly at the community level, mutiple resources must be considered. The most accessible knowledge available to most persons is at the community level, and it may well be at this level of involvement that significant learning takes place. Some suggested community exercises are recommended below, which can be carried out individually or with a group of persons.

1. What preventive health care programs for older persons presently exist in your community? In order to respond to this question, it will be necessary to visit your community health department and office on aging.
2. Plan to visit your community office on aging and discuss services to older persons.
3. Schedule a visit to a community nutrition site funded under Title VII of the Older Americans Act. After the visit, record your observations.
4. Conduct a study of how revenue-sharing funds in your community were spent during the past year. Were any of these funds used to provide services to older adults? Local, county, and state governments should be able to provide this information.

Learning Resources for Each Chapter

Chapter 1: Becoming Old with Dignity

Goals:

1. To develop the theory that aging is a normal process.
2. To provide examples of successful aging.
3. To explore potentially creative activities in the later years of life.

Exercises:

1. Divide a group into two sections. Ask one section to brainstorm for a half-hour and develop a list of negative words or phrases they can recall being used to describe older persons. Ask the second group to develop a list of positive words or phrases. At the end of a half-hour ask each group to share their lists. Which group had the longer list? Why do they feel this was the case?
2. Ask each member of your group to be silent for five minutes. Each member is to concentrate during this time on one personal thought, feeling, or possession which brings them pleasure. After five minutes, ask members of the group to share their feelings. Then, ask the group to close their eyes again. This time, members should be told that whatever it was they thought about is going to be taken from them. After a few minutes, discuss their feelings and whether they find any relationship of these feelings to the losses experienced by many older persons.

Additional Reading:

Bellow, Saul. *Mr. Sammler's Planet.* New York: Viking Press, 1970.
Greenfield, Josh. *Harry and Tonto.* New York: Dutton, 1974.
Morris, Wright. *A Life.* New York: Harper and Row, 1973.
Stegner, Wallace. *All the Little Things Live.* New York: Viking Press, 1967.
White, Patrick. *The Eye of the Storm.* New York: Viking Press, 1974.

Chapter 2: Stereotypes and Realities of Aging

Goals:

1. To describe ways in which aging may be measured.
2. To explain the characteristics of a stereotype.
3. To list common stereotypes associated with aging.

4. To describe the older adult in terms of the categories of organizer and disorganizer.
5. To list five general characteristics of the aging population in the United States.
6. To interpret the developmental approach to aging.
7. To outline three crises which may arise in the later years of life.

Exercises:

1. During the course of television viewing for the week, observe the images of older persons which arise. Based on the observations, what impressions were you given about what it means to be old?
2. In a group, stage a debate on the following issue: Resolved —individuals should be asked to retire at the age of 65. Divide your group into those who favor and those who oppose this resolution (persons need not agree with their position, but for the sake of debate are required to defend or oppose the proposition). Each group is given fifteen minutes to prepare their argument. After the arguments are presented, discuss which position seemed more logical and persuasive.
3. Prepare a budget for yourself based on the following factors: (1) An annual income of $4500 (2) Homeowner in inner city in a house that is not properly insulated (3) Source of income is Social Security plus a very small pension (4) No present health problems, but limited in terms of physical activity. Prepare the budget for a 12-month period, indicating how much of the $4500 will be earmarked for housing, food, health care, utility costs, and other living costs. If the costs exceed available income, try to decide where living expenses can be reduced or income increased.

Additional Reading:

Blau, Zena Smith. *Old Age in a Changing Society.* New York: New Viewpoints, 1973.

de Beauvoir, Simone. *The Coming of Age.* New York: Warner Paperback Library, 1973.

Botwinick, Jack. *Aging and Behavior: A Comprehensive Integration of Research Findings.* Second Edition. New York: Springer Publishing Company, 1978.

Butler, Robert. *Why Survive? Being Old in America.* New York: Harper and Row, 1975.

Knopf, Olga. *Successful Aging. The Facts and Fallacies of Growing Old.* New York: Viking Press, 1975.

Chapter 3: The Psychology of Aging

Goals:

1. To describe four approaches to the study of behavior in the later years of life.
2. To explain the relationship between loss and aging.
3. To assess personality development in the later stages of life.

Exercises:

1. Make a list of what new roles for older persons, other than grandparent or volunteer worker, you would want to see developed.
2. As a member of an interviewing team, describe how you might consult with each of the following: the young-old, middle-old, and old-old.

Additional Reading:

Berezin, Martin A., and Cath, Stanley H. (Editors). *Geriatric Psychiatry: Grief, Loss and Emotional Disorders in the Aging Process.* New York: International Universities Press, 1965.

Birren, James E., and Schaie, K. Warner. *The Handbook of the Psychology of Aging.* New York: Van Nostrand Reinhold, 1977.

Birren, James E. *The Psychology of Aging.* Englewood Cliffs, N.J.: Prentice-Hall, 1964.

Botwinick, Jack. *Cognitive Processes in Maturity and Old Age.* New York: Springer, 1967.

Bromley, Dennis B. *The Psychology of Human Ageing.* Baltimore: Penguin Books, 1974.

Butler, Robert N., and Lewis, Myrna I. *Aging and Mental Health: Positive Psychosocial Approaches,* Second Edition. St. Louis, Missouri: Mosby, 1977.

Eisdorfer, Carl, and Lawton, M. Powell (Editors). *The Psychology of Adult Development and Aging.* Washington, D.C.: American Psychological Association, 1973.

Field, Minna. *Aging With Honor and Dignity.* Springfield, Illinois: Charles C. Thomas, 1968.

Kallish, Richard A. (Editor). *Dependencies of Old People.* Ann Arbor, Michigan: University of Michigan, 1969.

Kastenbaum, Robert. *New Thoughts on Old Age.* New York: Springer Publishing Company, 1964.

Chapter 4: The Wisdom of the Body

Goals:

1. To describe how aging affects the body.
2. To show the relationship between stress and the aging process.
3. To outline theories related to the aging of the body.

Exercises:

1. If technology were capable of slowing down the aging process—or even eliminating death—in what ways would social structures change?
2. Stage a debate on the following issue: Resolved—decreased sexual activity in the later years of life is directly related to cultural definitions of beauty.

Additional Reading:

Bakerman, Seymour (Editor). *Aging Life Processes.* Springfield, Illinois: Charles C. Thomas, 1969.

Burnet, F. M. *Biology of Aging.* New York: Oxford University Press, 1975.

Burnside, I. M. (Editor). *Sexuality and Aging.* Los Angeles: Andrus Gerontology Center, 1975.

Comfort, Alex. *The Biology of Senescence.* New York: Holt, Rinehart and Winston, 1964.

Curtis, Howard J. *Biological Mechanisms of Aging.* Springfield, Illinois: Charles C. Thomas, 1966.

Jonas, Steven. *Health Care Delivery in the United States.* New York: Springer Publishing Company, 1977.

Koestenbaum, Peter. *Existential Sexuality.* Englewood Cliffs, N.J.: Prentice-Hall, 1974.

Timeras, P. S. *Developmental Physiology and Aging.* New York: Macmillan, 1972.

Chapter 5: Social Values and the Aging Process

Goals:

1. To describe the history of social gerontology.
2. To interpret the major theories of social gerontology.
3. To consider roles which unfold in the later years of life.

Exercise:

1. Make a list of the traditional roles associated with old age. Explore what new roles older persons might fulfill in society

by discussing this question with older persons. What roles would they want to continue from the past? What new roles in the later years of life do they envision?

Additional Reading:

Atchley, Robert C. *The Social Forces in Later Life.* Belmont, California: Wadsworth Publishing Company, 1972.

Brim, Orville, and Wheeler, Stanton. *Socialization After Childhood.* New York: Wiley, 1966.

Cumming, Elaine, and Henry, William E. *Growing Old: The Process of Disengagement.* New York: Basic Books, 1961.

Kalish, Richard A. *Late Adulthood: Perspectives of Human Development.* Monterey, California: Brooks/Cole Publishing Company, 1975.

Kimmel, D. C. *Adulthood and Aging: An Interdisciplinary, Developmental View.* New York: Wiley, 1974.

Maas, H. S., and Kuypers, J. A. *From Thirty to Seventy.* San Francisco: Jossey-Bass, 1974.

Neugarten, Bernice (Editor). *Middle Age and Aging.* Chicago: University of Chicago Press, 1972.

Rosow, Irving. *Socialization to Old Age.* Berkeley, California: University of California, 1974.

Williams, Richard H., and Wirth, Claudine G. *Lives Through the Years.* New York: Atherton Press, 1965.

Chapter 6: Public Policies and the Older Person

Goals:

1. To understand the relationship between public policy and cultural values.
2. To define public policy.
3. To interpret the policies and titles of the Older Americans Act.

Exercise:

1. Conduct a survey of a few businesses and industries to determine their retirement policies.

Additional Reading:

Binstock, Robert H. *Political Consequences of Aging.* Philadelphia: American Academy of Political and Social Sciences, 1974.

Golembiewski, Robert T. (Editor). *Perspectives on Public Management.* Itasca, Illinois: F. E. Peacock Publishers, 1968.

Jones, Charles O. *An Introduction to the Study of Public Policy.* Belmont, California: Duxbury Press, 1970.

Lindblom, Charles E. *The Policy-Making Process.* Englewood Cliffs, N.J.: Prentice-Hall, 1968.

McKinney, John C., and de Vyver, Frank T. *Aging and Social Policy.* New York: Appleton-Century-Crofts, 1966.

U.S. Department of Health, Education and Welfare, Administration on Aging. *The Older Americans Act of 1965, As Amended.* DHEW Publication No. 75-20170, December 1974.

Waldo, Dwight. *The Study of Public Administration.* New York: Random House, 1955.

Chapter 7: Planning Programs for Older Adults

Goals:

1. To describe goal-oriented planning and its relationship to the field of aging.
2. To describe the steps for setting up a systematic planning process.
3. To outline ways in which the needs of older persons can be assessed.

Additional Reading:

Each state is required to publish and make available a State Plan on Aging, which should be available from each state office on aging. In each region, a copy of an Area Plan on Aging should be available from the Area Agency on Aging.

Chapter 8: Community Development and the Network on Aging

Goals:

1. To explore the concept and process of community development.
2. To identify national priorities for older persons.
3. To identify the components of a national network on aging.
4. To explore ways in which older persons may be integrated into the mainstream of community life.

Additional Reading:

Banfield, Edward C. *The Unheavenly City.* Boston: Little, Brown and Company, 1970.

Cary, Lee J. (Editor). *Community Development As a Process.* Columbia: University of Missouri Press, 1970.

Gubrium, J. F. (Editor). *Late Life: Communities and Environmental Policy.* Springfield, Illinois: Charles C. Thomas, 1974.

Hardy, Richard E., and Cull, John G. *Organization and Administration of Service Programs for the Older American.* Springfield, Illinois: Charles C. Thomas, 1975.

Lawton, M. Powell, and Byerts, T. (Editors). *Community Planning for the Elderly.* Washington, D.C.: Gerontological Society, 1973.

Warren, Roland L. *Studying Your Community.* New York: The Free Press, 1965.

Chapter 9: Outreach and Communications with Older Persons

Goals:

1. To define the importance of outreach efforts in the field of aging.
2. To list the characteristics of a successful outreach program.
3. To outline the role and responsibility of outreach workers.

Additional Reading:

Bannon, Joseph J. *Outreach: Extending Community Service in Urban Areas.* Springfield: Illinois: Charles C. Thomas, 1973.

Ivey, Allen E. *Microcounseling.* Springfield, Illinois: Charles C. Thomas, 1971.

Schulman, Eveline D. *Intervention in Human Services.* St. Louis: C. V. Mosby, 1974.

Index